THE HEART OF ROCK AND ROLL

Nancy French

Mark Tucker

Tom Palmer

Aaron Rapoport

"*Make a joyful noise unto the LORD, all the earth: make a loud noise, and rejoice, and sing praise.*"

Psalms 98:4

Tom Wray

Ken Beebe

John Scarpati

Clockwise from upper left corner: Randy Stonehill, Amy Grant, Steve Taylor, Rez Band, Mylon LeFevre, Michael Omartian, Petra, Jessy Dixon, Stryper, Leslie Phillips.

Dan Du Verney

Harry Langdon

THE HEART OF ROCK AND ROLL

STEVE RABEY

Fleming H. Revell Company
Old Tappan, New Jersey

Photo Credits   John Barrett/Globe Photos: page 103; Ken Beebe: pages 12, 14, 16–17; John Bellissimo: page 44; Compassion International: pages 82, 83, 85, 86, 99; Dean Dixon: pages 40, 80, 89; Dan Du Verney: pages 32, 36; Nancy French: pages 46, 47, 90; Richard H. Heeren/Compassion International: page 87; Scott Herzer: page 79; Dennis R. Keitzman: pages 15, 19; Harry Langdon: page 52; Bernard Lemike: pages 20, 21, 94, 97; Tom Palmer: pages 24, 28, 70, 72, 75, 76, 78, 79; Neal Preston/PEOPLE Weekly/© 1986 Time, Inc.: page 105; Steve Rabey: pages 26, 34, 35, 67, 68, 69, 92, 95, 96, 98; Aaron Rapoport: pages 42, 49, 50, 51; Dick Randall: page 30; John Scarpati: pages 62, 64, 65, 66; Mike Tabor: page 25; Mark Tucker: page 100; Janet Vincent: page 39; Tom Wray: pages 22, 30.

Library of Congress Cataloging-in-Publication Data

Rabey, Steve.
    The heart of rock and roll.

    1. Christian rock music—United States—History
and criticism.   2. Rock music—United States—Religious
aspects—Christianity.   3. Rock musicians—United
States—Biography.   I. Title.
ML3187.5.R3   1986   783.6   86-10064
ISBN 0-8007-1483-0 (pbk.)

Copyright © 1986 by Steve Rabey
Published by the Fleming H. Revell Company
Old Tappan, New Jersey 07675
Printed in the United States of America

CONTENTS

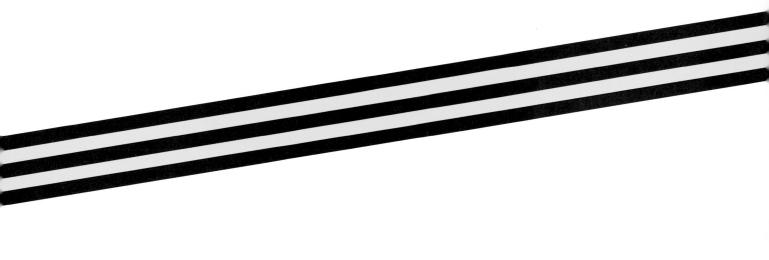

ACKNOWLEDGMENTS

Since this is my first book, there are a lifetime's worth of thank yous to make. Let me express my gratitude to:

—God, who enables me to live, breathe, *and* write;

—Claudia, my wife, who graciously gave up some of our time together so I could work on this project;

—Mom and Pop, whose enjoyment of music was infectious, and who always made me practice the piano;

—some super siblings—Sue, Phil, and Mike—who exposed me to Bob Dylan, Peter, Paul & Mary, and James Brown well before I reached the age of accountability;

—Grant Edwards, John Elliott, Marianne Struck, and others at the House Christian Fellowship who opened my eyes;

—Daved, for your friendship, talent, and the snazzy artwork;

—Charles and Elva Kip and Jay Weygandt at Logos of Springfield;

—Rob Marshall at Road Home;

—the fine English faculty members at Wright State University who gave me an education *and* a degree (and remember, you're responsible for this);

—the Vicars of Vinyl, Titans of Tape, and Courageous Defenders of Compact Discs, namely—

Scott Pelking at Word, Melissa Helm at Myrrh LA, and Karen Renfro at Myrrh;

Bob Angelotti and Marley Olson at Sparrow;

Rich Orienza at Enigma;

and Landra Chasteen at Benson;

—the folks at Compassion International and Covenant Presbyterian Church;

—the artists themselves, who found a place in their schedules and hearts to submit to lengthy and demanding interviews;

—and Marina Marketos and the Revell staff, who had the vision for this book.

INTRODUCTION

"Why should the devil have all the good tunes?" asked a preacher a century and a half ago.

A decade and a half ago Larry Norman asked the same question in his rock song, "Why Should the Devil Have All the Good Music?"

"Why indeed!" say the ten artists featured in this book. But they don't just sit around asking questions; they put their God-given talents to work making music with meaning. Take a look at

—Mylon LeFevre, a Southerner who was using rock music to sing about being born again before some of today's musicians were born the first time;

—Rez Band, hard-rock heirs of the Jesus Movement of the sixties and seventies and radical followers of Christ's example of caring for the meek and lowly of this world;

—Jessy Dixon, a talented and versatile musician who not only sings gospel music but now also believes wherein he sings;

—Leslie Phillips, a young singer/songwriter whose songs go boldly where Christian music has seldom trod before;

—Michael Omartian, a devoted Christian who helps artists like Rod Stewart and Jermaine Jackson create hit records;

—Stryper, a fearless foursome that takes the principle of ministering to people where they are to new and exciting heights;

—Steve Taylor, a "PK" (preacher's kid) whose biting satire and wild wit give new life to sometimes staid Christian concepts;

—Petra, a pioneering Christian band that has played to millions of attentive, happy listeners;

—Randy Stonehill, an intelligent lyricist, strong musician, and engaging performer whose songs can make you laugh and cry;

—and Amy Grant, who continues to take her polished pop-style gospel music to anyone who has ears to hear

These artists are busy making music that pleases the ear and challenges the heart. Music that holds out hope for more than a short-lived good time. Music that teams up timeless truths with timely tunes. Music that breaks down steely walls of disbelief and dazzles dead ears with good news about the Son of God.

But they weren't too busy to take a few hours to talk about their music and their calling.

We're glad they could, because now is the time for music like this. Christian young people aren't happy with a diet consisting only of "Amazing Grace," and unchurched listeners welcome an alternative to music of doom, despair, and depression.

And today is the day for this book. Not that yesterday would have been too soon, but now we can see some of the cumulative cultural effects of nearly two decades of Christian rock.

In 1985 contemporary Christian music first truly "crossed over," with Amy Grant and Stryper earning significant radio airplay, sales, and media coverage in the American mainstream.

Now more than ever, younger believers and their friends not only hear with their ears that Christ is relevant to twentieth-century mediums and messages, but can see with their eyes that Christian rock serves as a much needed salt in a modern entertainment industry that often promotes any sin that sells.

This new Christian music is cultural salt—not salt to hurt as it is rubbed into another's wounds, but salt that acts as a preservative of everything it touches.

Of course, some in the church still prefer the hymns, and that's okay. Others struggle with definitions: Is it rock? Is it roll? Does it harm your soul?

Still others speak in absolutes. They feel God has told them that rock must roll—back into the womb of hell where it was allegedly born.

With music, as with everything else in this life, we see through a glass darkly. It's been said that God and King David are planning an intensive seminar entitled The Real Absolute Truth About Music, but until then we have to grope along as best we can.

Perhaps this book can help us grope better, with more truth and more love. Perhaps it can let us see what makes some of these unique artists tick and how they view their calling to proclaim the Rock of Ages through the rock of this age.

It's not the only way to communicate truth but, as John Stott writes in *Involvement*, Volume I, it may be one way:

"From the pulpit, through letters to and articles in national and local newspapers, in discussions at home and at work, through opportunities in radio and television, by poetry and popular songs, we are called as Christians to witness to God's law and God's gospel, without fear or apology."

Amen.

MYLON LEFEVRE

For Mylon LeFevre, who started out singing southern gospel at the age of four and has since belted out both southern-fried and sanctified rock, much of the world of secular rock can be summed up in one incident.

It was 1973 and Mylon was in England with widely hailed British guitarist Alvin Lee. Alvin had grown both rich and disillusioned with his band, Ten Years After, which had stolen at least part of the show at the Woodstock rock festival in 1969.

Lee and LeFevre were recording their album, *On the Road to Freedom.* To do it up right they had purchased a fifteenth-century castle in Berkshire and, with the help of their road-ies, built a twenty-four-track recording studio there.

They invited some of their friends over to help on the album, and Steve Winwood of Traffic, Mick Fleetwood of Fleetwood Mac, Rolling Stones guitarist Ron Wood, King Crimson (later Foreigner) drummer Ian Wallace, Bad Company bassist Boz Burrell, and Beatle George Harrison (credited on the album as Hari Georgeson) accepted the invitation.

After all the guests left, Mylon and Alvin were polishing up a few of the album's cuts. They filled the area of the castle that held a swimming pool and tennis court with micro-phones and electronic gear, converting it into a heavily amplified echo chamber. As Lee played his guitar, Mylon listened at the control board—the two working together to cap-ture that perfect guitar feedback sound.

Mylon noticed strange noises coming over the studio monitor and checked some of the mikes to see what the problem was, but to no avail. The noises continued, and remained hidden.

As work on the song continued, Mylon realized something: Their noisy quest for the perfect sound was destroying the building. The roof of the tennis court was about to col-lapse. He alerted Lee to the problem and the two quickly got out of the way, but they didn't

Mylon (right) and road manager Clay Spivey taping PTL's Sound Effects" show.

have a spare second to salvage any of the thousands of dollars worth of equipment.

Recalling the incident today, Mylon views it through different eyes than he did then. "Babylon has fallen," he laughs, thinking of his years making a god of his music, the years before he knew Jesus.

Now God is God, and music is music.

Although he could still tell hundreds of anecdotes full of big-name celebrities and wild goings-on, he prefers, as Paul did two thousand years ago, to know one thing: Christ and Him crucified.

"I don't want to talk about all the foolish things I did in the past," he says in a slow, southern drawl that sounds like dark honey being poured from a jar. "I want to talk about what Jesus Christ has done for me since I began trusting Him."

That Old Gospel Ship

One would think that trusting God was something that would have come naturally to Mylon, who was born into a family that had been singing gospel music since 1921. The LeFevres were known throughout the South and elsewhere as a busy touring and recording gospel music institution.

Mylon got into the gospel swing of things at an early age, standing on a piano bench to reach the microphone in his first public performance at age four, and recording his first album when he was twelve. Soon he was writing the group's songs and arrangements and producing their albums. Before he left to perform his own southern-rock influenced brand of Christian music, Mylon recorded thirty-three albums with the LeFevres and the Stamps Quartet.

The first song Mylon wrote was "Without Him."

Without Him I could do nothing
Without Him I'd surely fail
Without Him I would be drifting
Like a ship without a sail

Jesus, Jesus
Do you know Him today
Please don't turn Him away
Jesus, my precious Jesus
Without Him how lost I would be

It was an immediate hit for the LeFevres and over the years other artists, including Elvis Presley, the Oak Ridge Boys, and Pat Boone, recorded the song. People still record "Without Him" today. It has appeared on 130 albums and still brings Mylon regular royalty payments.

But instead of growing up with a firm faith in Christ, Mylon grew rebellious and critical of the gospel music world and the people in it. "What I saw was a business," he says. "For me it really didn't have anything to do with ministry. The reason I was out on the road wasn't to lead people to Christ, it was to make a living. Things are totally different with me now, but the Lord has let me see that side of the fence."

After Elvis recorded "Without Him," Mylon became totally self-supporting: "I was in the Army making eighty-four dollars a month when Elvis did the tune. There I was, eighteen years old, and I received a royalty check for a small fortune. I had all this money and wondered, *What am I going to do with all of this?* Ninety days later another big wad came."

Mylon started spending money like crazy. He bought a Corvette, a boat, an apartment, and motorcycles. "I had spent fifteen thousand dollars, but there was nothing else I wanted," he says.

The sudden fame combined with his weak faith led to trouble. Some of his "extra" money began winding up in the hands of drug dealers as Mylon started experimenting with marijuana and other substances.

I didn't know that God was really God. It was like He was the Good Guy Upstairs. He wasn't somebody I could communicate with and who would let me know for sure He could handle my problems.

I believed in Him, because everyone told me Jesus was the Son of God. And I needed that fire insurance, because I didn't want to go to hell. But I didn't *really* believe. He was my Savior, but He wasn't the Lord of my life. I didn't know that you could really trust Him, so I didn't.

The first time I got high, I thanked God for marijuana. I wasn't happy and I just felt like I needed a break so bad.

Tensions began to develop between Mylon and his family. They didn't care for his life-style, and he wasn't happy working within the confines of southern gospel's country and four-part-harmony style. The argument came to a head—Mylon's head—over the length of his sideburns. In 1969 he left the group.

Although Mylon left the LeFevres, he didn't leave gospel music. Instead he gathered a group of musicians from the Atlanta, Georgia, area (some of the same musicians who later formed the popular band The Atlanta Rhythm Section) and recorded the world's second Christian rock album which was released on the secular Cotillion label in 1970. (Larry Norman had recorded the first, *Upon This Rock*, for Capitol in 1969.)

Mylon, as the album was called, was full of songs Mylon had been writing for years but which didn't fit the LeFevres' musical image. All the songs combined southern-fried rock with solid gospel lyrics.

The album opened with "Old Gospel Ship," a song that Mylon still plays in concert and which appears on his 1985 album with the band Broken Heart, *Sheep in Wolves Clothing*.

Other songs on that first album included "Sunday School Blues"

> *You've got to understand and appreciate what He's done for me and you*
> *Please don't get those Sunday school blues*

"Who Knows"

> *He knows how you feel, He knows what you say*
> *And He can lift you up and show you the way*
> *And with His love you can be saved*

"Sweet Peace Within"

> *There's one question I've got to ask you my friend*
> *What's gonna happen when you reach the end*
> *Are you going to have that sweet peace within*

and "You're Still on His Mind"

> *Think about that lonely day on cruel Calvary*
> *Think about the way He suffered death for you and me*
> *When you face reality I know that you will find*
> *That you were on His mind*

And that's only the first side!

So You Want to Be a Rock and Roll Star

Mylon was warmly received, and Mylon was popular enough to start touring the country and to sign a recording contract with Columbia Records.

Although Jesus still popped up in Mylon's music, these references grew less frequent. His faith wasn't getting any stronger, and the seductions of the world were attacking him from all sides.

The first Columbia album was a 1971 release entitled *Mylon and Holy Smoke*, named after Mylon's band. Although Christian influences still shone through on songs like "Railroad Angels" ("Just try to keep sweet Jesus on your mind"), there were differences from Mylon's earlier work.

First, Mylon was being pressured to stop singing the gospel. He had signed with a secular management company that was less than happy with the singer/songwriter's constant references to religion in his music. For one thing, the songs Mylon wrote for the second album were published in part by St. Lucifer Music Company, a name his manager had conjured up. Also, the cross Mylon had requested appear on the album cover appeared upside down—a sign of demonic worship. "It wasn't that way when I had the album designed," says Mylon.

Second, among Mylon's songs was one with the strange title "Holy Smoke Doo Dah Band," which announced Mylon's goal of making it big:

> *I'm just a poor boy down in Georgia*
> *I'm riding on a big jet plane*
> *I don't know what I'm doing here*
> *I guess I can't complain*
> *I'm just flying around this country*
> *I'm a banging on my guitar*
> *Telling anybody who will listen to me*
> *I wanna be a big rock and roll star*

The 1972 album *Over the Influence* contained a similar mixture of the sacred and the profane. Christian songs included "Working on a Building" and "Waymaker" (both of which appeared on Mylon's 1983 album with

Broken Heart, *Live Forever*) and a duet with Little Richard on Richard's song, "He's Not Just a Soldier" ("God has an army and it's still marching on / He's calling for soldiers so why don't you come").

But there was also a rollicking version of "Blue Suede Shoes," and the mournful ballad, "For the Record."

> *I don't feel satisfied*
> *The blues make a man feel like dying inside*
> *. . . That good rock and roll will set us all free.*

Mylon faced constant criticism for bringing religion into rock. Typical of such criticism was Nick Tosches' review of *Over the Influence* for *Rolling Stone* magazine. Tosches pretty much ignored the music on the album to express his personal revulsion for all things Christian.

He said Mylon was "a part of the whole Jesus creep movement" (which he wasn't) and then complained: "Two thirds of the songs on this album are totally devoid of any relation to the real world. No sex, no drugs, no booze, no cars, no worldly problems, no worldly happiness. Everything revolves around this _____ ghost Jesus."

The angry reviewer then asked: "How can any human possibly comprehend 'Blue Suede Shoes' and then turn

around and warble stuff like 'Jesus is a waymaker / One day He made a way for me'?"

But criticism or no, Mylon was becoming more popular. Holy Smoke appeared in larger concert halls (and held its own very nicely) with artists like the Who, Pink Floyd, Bob Seger, Jimi Hendrix, Traffic, Jethro Tull, Joe Cocker, Grand Funk, J. Geils Band, and lots of others.

"Can you imagine doing concerts with bands like Black Sabbath and the Grateful Dead, all the time playing Christian music?" asks Mylon now, remembering how crazy it all was.

With increased popularity came increased earnings. Mylon was now making seven to eight hundred thousand dollars a year. And his taste in drugs had graduated too—from marijuana to cocaine to heroin.

Mylon's stage appearance grew more outlandish: He was covered in "leathers, feathers, furs, and bones." But as wild and crazy as things were becoming and in spite of the fog that surrounded Mylon's life, he still had at least a small part of his heart set on God.

"We never went on stage without praying," he says. "Most of the time we were high, but I remember praying, *Lord, please don't let me die in my sin. I need help. Help me, in Jesus' name.*"

Mylon also gave his testimony during concerts, and among those to be touched by what he said was Dana Key of DeGarmo & Key. Key gave his life to the Lord shortly after hearing Mylon in concert in Memphis.

"If Dana or anybody else had come backstage and talked to me, he would have decided that he didn't want any part of the life I was leading," says Mylon. "But on stage it was the Word of God, and the Word of God is still the Word of God, even if a donkey is telling it. It never comes back void."

My Heart Belongs to Him

Mylon's career as a rocker and his avoidance of God continued. "I had dreamed about doing all this stuff," he says of the fame and glory and money, "and my dreams started coming true."

Meanwhile, references to God appeared less frequently on his 1973 album with Alvin Lee and on his following solo albums: *Weak at the Knees* (1977), *Love Rustler* (1978), and *Rock & Roll Resurrection* (1979).

Oh, *Weak at the Knees* included the gospel-influenced "Understand It" ("If I can't turn to You, Jesus, who can I turn to?"), and a version of the gospel standard "Old Ship of Zion." And *Love Rustler* contained songs by Kerry Livgren of Kansas, Jeff Pollard of Le Roux, and Robin Lane, now three well-known names in Christian music. But Mylon didn't know Pollard and Lane, and Livgren hadn't yet met Christ.

Mylon's producers were telling him to cut out the religion and beef up the rock. But under the surface—and in Mylon's heart—things were churning.

For one thing, Mylon had contributed background vocals to Phil Keaggy's 1976 album, *Love Broke Thru.* This was his first contribution to a Christian album in a long time. "Before that I hadn't had any real communication with Christians," he says. "They just put me down." But at the Keaggy sessions the three members of Second Chapter of Acts, who were also singing on the album, and, in particular, producer Buck Herring, showered Mylon with love.

"In the long run," says Mylon, "when I figured it out, I knew I wanted to be more like those people who were dying to self, who were learning to be more and more like Jesus and less and less self-important. You could see what their lives stood for rather than who they were."

Mylon also had a close brush with death. In the early seventies a heroin overdose made his heart stop—and opened up his eyes. "That scared me," he says in understatement.

> Do you know how many friends have been buried since I became a rock and roller? Duane Allman and Berry Oakley of the Allman Brothers, Jimi Hendrix, Elvis, Ronnie Van Zant of Lynyrd Skynyrd, Keith Moon of the Who, Al Wilson of Canned Heat, Keith Godchaux of the Grateful Dead, on and on.
>
> I have been to so many funerals where people were buried with a joint in their mouth or a spoon in their nose—and they were really serious.
>
> All of a sudden I took a look at my life. I had wanted to burn bright and then when I was really high or something, just die. But I realized when I met death up close that I wasn't ready to meet God. I didn't want Him to judge me. I wanted time to look this thing over. Were all my sins forgiven? I wanted to know for sure.

So Mylon was given another chance to make things right with God. But another reason for the change in Mylon's life was the change that occurred in his father Urias's life right before he died.

> My father had always been a harsh person. He was six feet four inches tall, weighed more than two hundred fifty pounds, and was very authoritative. I loved him but I didn't like him.

> But then about three or four years before he died he started getting to know the Lord better. He became a real kind, caring, and gentle man. I asked him what was happening and he said, "It's just Jesus."
>
> I asked the Lord not to let me wait until I was dying to come to know Him. If Jesus could take one of the hardest men I ever knew and turn him into the kindest man I've ever known, I wanted to know that love too.

Mylon finally gave up the struggle, privately giving his heart to Jesus in 1979.

It's the kind of struggle that was described in the song "My Heart Belongs to Him" which appeared on *More* by Mylon and Broken Heart:

> *My mind has been a battlefield,*
> *where many wars were fought*
> *My soul has been a marketplace,*
> *where others sold and bought*
> *But through the lonely, wasted years*
> *There's One who knew my hidden fears*
> *And noticed the unnoticed tears*
> *Now my heart belongs to Him*

Musicians With a Mission

Mylon started out singing southern gospel music. He then served as one of the fathers of Christian rock. During the seventies he pursued rock more than his faith.

Today he has come full circle. Since 1981 he has been putting the gospel message to music. And instead of suffering from the "Sunday School Blues," he is an elder in Atlanta's thriving Mount Paran Church of God.

> Rock and roll could have killed me. When I gave my life to the Lord, I gave up music. It was too important to me. It was an idol. It was the way I got a lot of attention, and I was addicted to that attention.
>
> But God showed me, "I don't care about your music. I can make the stones and the rocks praise me. Every knee will bow someday, whether they like it or not. You're the one who has the problem with rock and roll. I don't really want or need it, all I want is your heart. But now that your heart is right about it, go on and rock."

Mylon didn't just step out of the secular spotlight and into the religious spotlight. He spent four years studying the Bible and waiting for direction from the Lord, under

Mylon, who's been thrilling crowds since he was four, is a favorite at the annual Creation festivals.

Mylon and Broken Heart (*left to right*): Paul Joseph (keyboard), David Payton (guitar), Mylon, Kenny Bentley (bass), Ben Hewitt (drums), and Scott Allen (guitar).

the guidance of Dr. Paul Walker, senior pastor of Mount Paran Church of God in Atlanta, Georgia.

"Also, at the time of my father's death, I felt I needed not only a spiritual leader but also someone to be a father figure to me," says Mylon. "Dr. M. G. McLuhan, Mount Paran's associate pastor, has been a friend, a brother, and a spiritual leader. I submit my spiritual life to him because he is discipling me. He is just pouring the Word of God into my heart."

As Mylon studied the Word he came across some musicians who shared his faith and ambitions. But even though he had played with Eric Clapton and other musical luminaries, Mylon didn't select the members of his band, Broken Heart, on the basis of talent.

God showed me the heart of each of these guys. He told me each of them should be in the band because they knew Him and loved Him. They knew who created talent—they prayed for talent and worked hard.

We had very humble beginnings. We weren't very good. None of the guys had ever been in a professional band, but we worked hard. We weren't getting any bookings so we played at prisons, hospitals, and schools around Atlanta. It was during that time that we started learning how

God does things, and the whole time the pastors at Mount Paran were discipling us.

In order to keep eating and learn humility we worked as janitors at the church. Ben Hewitt worked as the church's yardman, while Kenny Bentley, our bassist, and Scott Allen, our guitarist, and I worked as janitors. We each got seventy-five dollars a week, the band got a great place to rehearse, and they would give us time off if we had to go play a gig.

It's been rough, but this is not a career for us—it's a ministry.

Now Broken Heart is sounding more professional, and requests for the band to play come more frequently. The band plays an average of two hundred concerts a year, all over the country.

Although their concerts are well-attended and their recordings are selling at a brisk pace, Mylon isn't making the kind of money he made—or could make again—playing secular rock. But there are greater rewards of another variety.

"Tonight fourteen people came to know Jesus," he says after a recent concert. "Compared to that, what is fifty thousand dollars, or any amount of money?"

In this and many other ways Mylon and the other members of Broken Heart still view their music as a ministry, as they sing in a song called "The Warrior" from the *Sheep in Wolves Clothing* album:

> *Many years on the road*
> *Many more miles to go*
> *We cannot waste another single day*
> *The nights are hard and long*
> *But He has made us strong enough*
> *To take His love and give it all away*
> *And I know—He said to go*
>
> *'Cause there's a war that's going on, a soul is raging*
> *A battle weary warrior is praying*
> *And you must understand what the song is saying*
> *Come on home to the Father*
> *Come on home to the Son*
> *Come on home the battle's over, Christ has won.*

In 1985, Broken Heart took the message of redemption to the airwaves, as the band's video for the song "Stranger to Danger" aired on MTV and other national shows. The song sings of being lost and being found:

I'm no stranger to danger
But I'm brand new in love
And it's the last of the past
That I'm finally free of
I was a child of the wild
Until Your love set me free
I'm no stranger to danger
But I'm gonna be

The well-produced video portrays the Holy Spirit as riding on a motorcycle seeking out Mylon, who is pictured as a lost, tormented soul. Ultimately, Mylon heeds the call and invites others to follow too. The song closes with Mylon and the band singing, "I'm gonna be like Jesus."

Dr. McLuhan, the associate pastor at Mount Paran, knows the band members fight as spiritual warriors. He sees them every Tuesday morning at the Bible studies he leads with the band and crew. That's why he retired at the end of 1985 to devote more time to the ministry of Broken Heart. Dr. McLuhan explains:

These guys combine a first-class concert with a very powerful evangelistic appeal. I understand what they're doing. It's like Paul, who said that he would be all things to all people in order that he might win some. The band is reaching kids who are not going to come into a normal church.

Of course, there has been some criticism of the band, both in the church and in the community. But some influential people in the community began to support us when their kids, who were involved in drugs, came to know the Lord through the concerts here. We look upon the group as a very viable outreach for this congregation.

And Mylon looks at the church as a viable home for the band.

"I have no doubt in my mind that the Lord placed me in Mount Paran Church in Atlanta, Georgia," says Mylon, who besides being an elder is called Director of Outreach Ministry. "It has put me in balance and my entire life has changed.

"There are sixteen families in the Broken Heart ministry, and we all go to the same church. We receive the same spiritual food, and we're thinking about, praying about, and studying the same things. So when somebody comes up to us at a concert and asks what God's Word says about something, they don't get three different answers. They're going to get one version, one vision."

It's been a long and rocky road for Mylon, but now he knows that he is on the road to somewhere rather than nowhere.

Where's John Bonham of Led Zeppelin? He's just dead. Or Brian Jones of the Stones? And John Lennon? And where's Elvis? He may have been the king of rock and roll, but he's dead. All these guys are either in heaven or hell, because there isn't anywhere else to go.

What it all comes down to is that there's just one King—the King of Kings and the Lord of Lords, and that's the only game in town.

And I want to serve that King with all my heart and soul and mind. I want to live in such a way that God can enjoy me as much as I enjoy Him, because I have fallen in love with Jesus.

Wendi and Glenn Kaiser during the shooting of their video for "Love Comes Down."

Chapter Two

REZ BAND

The crowd at Chicago's Odeum auditorium is frenzied. Thousands of people are standing, their hands waving in the air. Rez Band, a group that has been playing in and around Chicago for thirteen years, is midway through its set.

Guitarist Glenn Kaiser and drummer John Herrin, both pastors in a local Christian community, are leading a rhythmic assault on the ears and bodies of the people in the audience.

Glenn slashes at his guitar like he's fighting off a six-stringed attacker, while John throws his sticks at his drums. Stu Heiss on guitar and Jim Denton on bass add their instruments to the musical mix. Then Wendi Kaiser belts out her harsh vocals to the first verse of a song that paints a bleak picture of the emptiness of modern life:

> *Hiding out in my bedroom*
> *I wish that I could die*
> *No one seems to love me*
> *But I'm not going to cry*

The band completes the verse and heads for the chorus:

> *I hate it here in Area 312*
> *Can't make it here in Area 312*
> *Operator, listen please*
> *I got this loneliness disease*
> *In Area 312*

It's not like the hymns and religious ditties people sing in church, but then Rez Band—short for Resurrection Band—is not singing to church people.

As part of Jesus People USA, a unique group of some five hundred people who live in Christian community in Chicago's inner city, the members of Rez Band are only too aware that many in their audience have experienced the emptiness and sadness expressed in the song "Area 312," which is named for Chicago's area code.

The people of JPUSA (which they pronounce, "juh-poo'-zuh") live in the midst of a city of more than 3 million people, many with empty stomachs, empty pockets, and empty hearts.

A lot of Chicago's young street people come to Rez Band concerts, attracted by the band's uncompromising rock sound.

Yet, even in the midst of Windy City's urban ghetto, and even in the midst of a song like "Area 312," Rez Band sees a ray of hope. In the song's third verse are the words:

> *Feeling so distressed tonight*
> *Jesus, are You there*
> *Could we talk a little while*
> *I heard You really care*

And at the end of this particular concert, which was etched in vinyl for posterity on the live album *Bootleg*, Glenn Kaiser delivers a hip, penetrating invitation: "You can go to any library. You can see that Jesus Christ lived. There's no question that He's real. But the question for so many of us tonight is, Are we real? Are we real with Him?"

As in most other concerts, the message of the music and the invitation was heard. Young people came forward to give their lives to God, drawn to the gentle Savior by harsh-sounding, intense rock and roll.

Street Beat

Home base for Rez Band is JPUSA's main building on Chicago's north side. Visiting there is like taking a trip back in time—either to the heyday of the Jesus Movement of the 1970s, or to the first days of the Christian church as portrayed in the Bible's Book of Acts.

Like many people who found Christ during the Jesus Movement, the people at JPUSA are dressed in a variety of counterculture getups. Some sport long hair; many wear clothes that would insure more than a few nasty stares at most American churches.

In fact, the core of the group that started JPUSA came from a group called Jesus People of Milwaukee that was

Rez Band (*left to right*): Jim Denton, John Herrin, Stu Heiss, Wendi Kaiser, and Glenn Kaiser.

founded in the early seventies. JPUSA is a living historical artifact, being the only Christian community of any size to survive from the period that spawned what a 1971 *Time* magazine cover story called the "Jesus Revolution."

Glenn Kaiser, John Herrin, and four others who now serve as pastors of JPUSA went to Florida in 1972 as part of a traveling missionary outreach of the Milwaukee Jesus People. From Florida they went to Chicago for a series of concerts and visits to friends. The concerts kept on coming, with each booking leading to another booking down the road.

The organization set up house in inner-city Chicago in 1973, and they've been there ever since.

JPUSA also has many similarities to first-century Christians. Like the early believers, the group in Chicago "has all things in common." More than 350 adults and 125 kids live in community in several old Chicago buildings. Many of them hold jobs with one of the organization's businesses (JP Roofing, JP Carpentry, JP Moving, JP Graphics, etc.), but none of them has any money!

Members earn money, but they don't keep it for themselves. Their earnings go into a central purse, and members' personal needs are cared for from the common funds.

"What we're dealing with here is Acts, chapter 2, and Acts, chapter 4," says Glenn Kaiser, leader of Rez Band and one of ten pastors of JPUSA.

We're very close to the poverty level. We buy bulk and share whatever profits there are. We feel a call to this kind of life-style. We feel we can accomplish so much more.

It wouldn't make sense for us to be rich and live in the inner city because it would be like commuting. The people God has given us to reach and minister to in our own neighborhood would be given such ammunition to reject Jesus Christ because of these hypocrisies, so we reject that kind of attitude.

The struggle of all of us in the community is to—as they say—live on the need level and not the greed level. We are fighting to maintain a standard of living and life-style that will continue to validate the gospel we are preaching to the poor.

But the people of JPUSA don't just preach to the poor—they feed them.

Every day around noontime the line starts to form outside the old hotel on North Malden Avenue that houses most of the JPUSA members. As the line grows longer

Rez Band and other members of JPUSA live out their faith by feeding Chicago's hungry.

you can see street people of every imaginable (and even unimaginable) variety: gray old men in tattered outfits, young men who look employable but who have "dropped out" of society, and bag ladies of all sizes and ages.

By one o'clock in the afternoon two to three hundred people are waiting in line. The doors to the JPUSA open, the street people stream in, and they eat—after a brief prayer of thanks to God. After the meal they can pick up clothing the Jesus People have gathered for them.

This scene is repeated every day, 365 days a year.

Okay. But what's this got to do with the Rez Band?

Just like every other "business" of JPUSA, the earnings from Rez Band's concerts (the band plays approximately eighty-five concerts for more than one hundred twenty-five thousand people every year) and recordings (the band has eight albums and has sold more than half a million records) go into the common purse that feeds not only JPUSA members but also Chicago's street people.

Songs to Raise the Dead

JPUSA has a number of ministries that resemble those seen during the Jesus Movement. The organization publishes *Cornerstone*, a bimonthly magazine that is more stimulating and professional than other publications of the once-flowering Christian underground press.

The Holy Ghost Players put the gospel into dramatic form—acting out biblical stories and truths at JPUSA's weekly worship services and around the city and the country. And all of the members—whether at work or at play—seem to have a burning desire to evangelize everyone they meet.

Like these other outreaches of JPUSA, the music Rez Band plays reflects the fellowship's practice of being in, but not of, the world as well as its members' commitment to saving the lost.

One can see the group's love for the poor, the troubled, and the criminal in the music video to the song "Crimes" from the band's 1984 release, *Hostage*. Sung by Wendi Kaiser, Glenn's wife of fourteen years, the song explores the world of street-wise kids and holds out a ray of hope.

> *It don't matter what they taught you*
> *When you're unemployed*
> *Feelin' restless and ripped off*
> *And you know you're annoyed*
>
> *I got a new piece of news for you*
> *You can get bailed out*
> *God can change your criminal heart*
> *That's what love's about.*

Even as early as 1978 on their debut album, *Awaiting Your Reply*, the songs were addressing the lost and weary people the band members saw all around them.

In "Waves," Glenn sang:

> *We see wave after wave*
> *Of people in the street*
> *Playing their songs, but*
> *Missing the beat.*

And 1980's *Colours* contained several street songs, from "City Streets"

> *You saw me standing out in the street*
> *I was looking for some action, someone to meet*
> *There was holes in my pockets and a hole in my soul*
> *And a whole lot of questions about which way to go*

to "N. Y. C."

> *In a New York City project another victim sits*
> *Her life is lost in being tossed down streets of trash and brick*

to "Amazing," which shows how God gives help to the homeless and lost.

> *You put me up, when life put me down*
> *You took me in, when sin shut me out*
> *You called my name when I felt forgotten*

"Stark/Spare" from *Mommy Don't Love Daddy Anymore* (1981), attacks the standard middle-class tactic of ignoring the poor,

Stark/spare and barely there
The ghetto moves beyond the knowledge
Or even consideration
Of the upper-middle riddles

but then counters that willful ignorance with the calling of Christ.

And God have mercy
On the rest of us too
'Cause when we shut out the poor
Lord, we're shutting out You.

It's not just lost adults who tug at these Chicago Christians' hearts either. In "Playground" from *Bootleg,* Wendi sings about the children who suffer the consequences of sinful adults.

I see them every day
With holes all in their clothes
Dirty faces, matted hair
Snot running from their nose

I wonder what they had to eat
I wonder where they sleep
Glue bags, porn, and suicide
The devil sells you cheap

The music that Rez Band uses to drive home these lyrics is no less direct than the words themselves. Although many have called the band's music heavy metal, Glenn Kaiser, who has written most of the material, prefers to call it "very intense hard rock."

Together, the words and music make for one of the most powerful sounds in Christian music. Says Glenn,

When we as a band write lyrics or songs, we have never dealt with it on the level of whether we will get airplay or whether the Christians will love us or hate us for it. From day one there has been a level of integrity—spiritually as well as artistically—that we have been praying and striving to maintain.

We would certainly like the non-Christian or the backslider to come to one of our concerts or to hear one of our records and accept it at face value. We want it to be that strong, that valid, that potent.

We look at ourselves as a band that just happens to be Christian. We are Christians first, and we make no bones about the fact that we follow Jesus and that we are speaking from a biblical perspective. But at the same time we are no longer afraid to be known as rock and roll musicians.

But Glenn, what about those who say rock is the devil's music?

We don't feel that there's any biblical basis for saying this style or that style of music is inherently evil. There's no biblical basis for that kind of argument.

And if we're not talking about biblical morality, and if we're not citing specific Scriptures that clearly speak about these things, then really all we're doing is tossing out our own opinions.

We feel that out of the abundance of the heart the mouth speaks. Whatever is in you is going to come out. If Jesus Christ is really our Lord and is really the center of our lives, then whether we're driving a Caterpillar tractor, playing pro baseball, playing in a rock and roll band, or standing behind a pulpit, this is all going to be evident.

Kaiser and Rez Band have taken their share of criticism for their uncompromising rock and their unshakable faith that God can use all kinds of music. Among their loudest critics is Texas evangelist and writer David Wilkerson.

Although he was once deeply involved in the same Jesus Movement that gave birth to Jesus People USA, and even wrote a brochure in defense of Christian rock, Wilkerson has now parted ways with bands like Rez Band. Wilkerson now declares that Christian rock is demonic, and that the Jesus People's dedication to their music caused God to withdraw His Holy Spirit from the whole movement.

Late in 1985, Kaiser met with Wilkerson at the evangelist's Lindale, Texas, office. As he told *Contemporary Quarterly*, the publication of the Fellowship of Contemporary Christian Ministries, the visit was an unhappy one:

"David Wilkerson is sincere. And wrong," wrote Kaiser. "I spent twenty minutes on the freeway crying my eyes out . . . God have mercy on a man we love who will hurt thousands who have never heard the gospel for lack of a vehicle to hear it!"

Most of the time, though, Kaiser isn't taking his ideas about Christian music to theological debates; he's taking the music to the streets.

We Play Because We Have To

Glenn Kaiser and the other members of Rez Band enjoy playing. You know that when you see them in concert: They throw themselves into the music more than they would if they were just out there doing a job.

But as much as they enjoy it, they wouldn't be playing rock music unless they felt God had called them to do so. As Glenn says:

Something a lot of people fail to understand or believe is that we're under orders. I didn't beseech God and say, "Can I please play in a Christian rock band?" The band was formed because the pastors in the fellowship in Milwaukee thought there needed to be a group that would play music that would relate to the kids the Lord had called us to reach.

After much prayer and fasting and a lot of counsel from different leaders, the band was put together as an outreach of the Milwaukee fellowship on December 14, 1971. At first we were called Charity, but the name was changed to Resurrection Band in 1972.

The mission of the band was confirmed to us through signs and wonders right away. At the very first concert a bunch of kids gave their hearts to Jesus Christ, and it has just snowballed through the years.

All along the way, I don't know what we would have done if we hadn't seen the fruit we saw. You hear those stories about missionaries who are off in a far away country for fifteen years and they never see anyone come to the Lord.

Sure there have been dry times—both as individuals and as a band—but by and large it has been a rare occasion for us to do a concert where people have not repented of their sins and invited Christ into their lives, or where Christians who are backsliding haven't prayed and asked God's forgiveness.

Perhaps one reason God can use Rez Band is because the band members have devoted their lives to serving Him, and one of the best symbols of this dedication is their dedication to their families and brothers and sisters in Chicago.

Glenn and Wendi have four children, while Jim Denton, John Herrin, and Stu Heiss are all married with two children each. Unlike secular or Christian bands that spend hundreds of days per year on the road, Rez Band tours only a few days at a time during a few months out of the year.

"We don't do as many concerts as some bands," says Glenn. "Typically we play for a few nights and then take time off to be involved in fellowship, take care of our families, attend to other areas of the ministry, or be involved in counselling or teaching with the fellowship."

The band's love for God can also be seen in their songs of praise and worship. In the title song from the 1980 *Colours* album, Glenn sings:

> *As the planets dance around the sun*
> *I rejoice in the risen One*
> *You are the Lord, the love of my life*
> *I wait for You in the morning light*

And in "The Struggle" from the same album, Glenn's lyrics show a soul standing naked before God.

> *Sometimes You scare me*
> *By what You cause me to see*
> *And I'm afraid of knowing who I am*
> *Although You've changed me*
> *There's still a whole lot of old wineskin*
> *And to open up would destroy the*
> *Me I'm afraid to show*

On *Hostage* the band performs "It's You," a song of love and adoration for God by fellowship member Jon Trott:

> *It's You*
> *Makes the atoms dance*
> *It's You*
> *Creates pure romance*
> *It's You*
> *I am thinking of*
> *It's You, You, You*

These and other Rez Band songs show that God lives in the midst of the JPUSA community living out its faith in Chicago's inner city.

Confronting the World

Rez Band's music can be directed toward God or it can be directed toward lost souls. But much of the band's recorded music provides a Christian critique of modern life.

Although those in the church may not like it, some of the band's songs are directed at the church's problems. In Jim Denton's composition "Who's Real Anymore," Wendi sings for those who wonder about televangelists:

> *Preachers beggin' on the radio*
> *Makin' pleas on TV shows—all right*
> *All I hear is gimme gimme money*
> *Isn't that a little bit funny—all right*

I know what you're thinkin'
I know what you're makin' of this
Who's real anymore

Colours features the song "An American Dream," which looks through some of the holes in our nation's civil religion.

The holy morning paper / Slaps the steps at dawn
America's doors open / Let's see what's going on
Confusion with our coffee / Fear and frosted flakes
The dollar takes another dive / Another bubble breaks

But the band's longest journey through cultural criticism is found on *Mommy Don't Love Daddy Anymore*. The title song shows the breakdown of a family and the effects on one family member:

Me I don't know who to believe
Me I don't know how to maintain

"Elevator Muzik" attacks America's consumerist creed:

Plastic muzik plastic food
Cellophane tunes for that
Synthetic mood . . .
Who cares if you like it
BUY IT!

Hostage contains the blistering song, "Defective Youth"—

We are twisted / We are rotten
No 60s answers, please
We are handsome / We are modern
Got a terminal social disease

Defective youth!
Why won't you listen

But as the last verse of the song reveals, maybe we are part of the reason the youth and others are on the wrong track:

You say He's the solution
You tell me you got love
I say you gotta prove it
When push comes to shove

Rez Band's musical and lyrical attack was even sharper on the 1985 album, *Between Heaven 'n' Hell*. "Zuid Afrikan" attacked apartheid, and "Walk On" retold the parable of the Good Samaritan in a realistic modern setting.

Two new songs took a distant look at this crazy planet. One—"2,000"—asked sad questions:

In the year two thousand
Will we still have minds
Will our hearts be stone cold

While "Nervous World" took a loving and critical look at a popular modern approach to life:

Why worry 'bout tomorrow
Let the good times roll
Big deal, if you reap what you sow
Why hurry through today
If you think it don't matter
And you don't really care where you go

In addition, "Love Comes Down," a powerful and thoroughly modern song about the hound of heaven, was made into a video that debuted on MTV in the spring of 1986.

No Ivory Tower Here

Rez Band, along with the hundreds of others who live with them at Jesus People USA headquarters in Chicago, have made a choice—to stay in the streets and live close to people in need.

Their approach hasn't been to live in cloistered seclusion while the distant world falls apart without them. Rather, they are urban guerrillas, fighting godly battles in the heart of the big metropolis.

And in their neighborhood, push often comes to shove.

An ad in *Cornerstone* recruiting believers for JPUSA's summer witnessing work read: "Summertime in Chicago . . . hot in more ways than one. When temperatures and tempers rise past the boiling point and hate and violence are forced out into the streets."

Rez Band and the other members of JPUSA are seeking to help their city through music, magazines, drama, witnessing, and other activities. But their most valued and desperately needed contributions to their city and their world is a vibrant, living testimony to the reality of God's love.

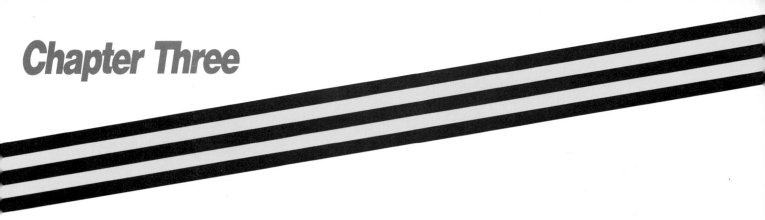

Chapter Three

JESSY DIXON

Jessy Dixon's rich, penetrating voice and dazzling keyboard work have been heard in stadiums, college auditoriums, and churches around the world. Raised in a family where combining music and religion was as natural as learning to walk, Jessy began playing at worship services in his native Texas during his teens.

In later years he added his talents to recording sessions at the world-renowned Chess Records studios in Chicago; to concerts and recordings by the man they call the Crown Prince of Gospel, James Cleveland; and to the music of pop artist Paul Simon, with whom Jessy toured for eight years.

Along the way he has recorded nearly twenty records, received three gold albums (for sales of more than half a million copies each), and pulled down a handful of Grammy nominations.

Certainly, this is a man who has been blessed by God.

But for many years Dixon's beautiful and inspiring voice hid a man with a confused heart. Early in his career Dixon sang gospel songs with skill and feeling, but he had not yet come to a personal understanding of what the gospel was about.

Or, as he told one writer, "My singing was anointed, but I wasn't."

Today things are different, as both Dixon's career and his life are dedicated to serving God. Now he not only sings the gospel, he believes it, lives it, and teaches it.

Jessy has already had an exciting and varied career in which he has been equally comfortable belting out spirituals to either largely black audiences of believers or mostly white audiences of Paul Simon fans.

In singing the gospel to the unchurched, Jessy was a pioneer in a field now dominated by artists like Amy Grant and Stryper. But now, all that behind him, Jessy is concentrating on body ministry—devoting his impressive talents to encouraging and building up believers worldwide.

protégé of James Cleveland) are just a few of the people who left the world of gospel music to make names, and even fortunes, for themselves singing pop, soul, and rock.

Jessy Dixon came from similar roots, but he didn't "sell out." He has remained a gospel artist all his life. Inspiring and preparing him for his life of singing God's praise were two important elements of his home—music and the church.

To Jessy, one of five Dixon children, music has always been very important, even as a child growing up in San Antonio, Texas.

> I can remember as a little boy that religion and music were both very important. Some of my first impressions are of me lying down on a pew in church asleep while my grandmother was dancing around me.
>
> Then my mother started giving me piano lessons when I was five. I was playing pieces by Rachmaninoff, Bach's Two-Part Inventions, and other things. I loved it. My father played piano and mandolin around the house a lot. He wanted me to play music too, but he wanted me to play secular, because he said I'd never make any money playing in the church.

In 1985 Jessy recorded his album *Silent Partner* and began touring with DeGarmo & Key, resulting in some of his best work in decades. The partnership reacquainted many listeners with this amazing singer. Others who heard him for the first time—either in concert or on "Destined to Win," his duet with Dana Key—came away stunned by his talent and conviction.

But Jessy has been singing beautifully about God for years.

"Have You Heard Jessy?"

The history of American music would be much different—and much shorter—if it weren't for the hundreds of black artists who spent years training their voices in churches throughout this land.

All those who say today's rock is the devil's music try to forget it, but one of the major contributions to the creation of rock music was made by black gospel singers. As Anthony Heilbut says in his definitive study of black gospel, *The Gospel Sound*, "All rock's most resilient features, the beat, the drama, the group vibrations derive from gospel."

Marvin Gaye, Gladys Knight, Curtis Mayfield, Sam Cooke, the Pointer Sisters, Lou Rawls, Ashford and Simpson, and Aretha Franklin (who, like Jessy, was a

Jessy took a middle ground between those who pushed him to play only in the church and others who encouraged a more secular career. He would show up faithfully every Sunday in church, ready to handle the organ- or piano-playing responsibilities. Meanwhile, he would attend concerts by Ray Charles, Little Richard, and other emerging blues and rock performers who came through the San Antonio area.

And as the seemingly contradictory influences of classics, hymns, and rock played inside Jessy's mind, he developed a unique style of playing and singing that combined all these styles.

Then, one Sunday, something happened that would occur repeatedly in Jessy's life. Someone heard Jessy play, and opportunity knocked.

This time it was the daughter of a Chicago preacher who heard Jessy as he played for the believers at Antioch Baptist Church in San Antonio. She called her father, Reverend Paxton of Chicago's True Light Baptist Church, and told him she had heard the organist the church needed. Paxton came and heard the then-teenaged Jessy for himself and decided he wouldn't leave Texas unless he had the phenomenal organist with him.

"He came to Texas to get me," says Jessy. "He asked my mother if I could come to Chicago. He promised he would take care of me and keep me out of trouble."

Jessy (right) and Dana Key shared vocals on "Destined to Win."

Jessy wasn't in the Windy City long when it happened again. Before he knew it, somebody else heard him play and liked what they heard.

True Light Baptist had a radio broadcast every Sunday, and music was an important part of the church. My style was different from other organists in Chicago. I played bluesy I guess.

Pretty soon, other musicians—secular as well as gospel—came to hear me play. I came up from Texas hearing Ray Charles and Little Richard, and I guess I thought everybody played like that.

Jessy spent five years at True Light Baptist and, over that period, hundreds of people heard him. Among them were two people who would take Jessy closer to fame and acclaim—Reverend James Cleveland and Chess Records founder Leonard Chess.

"James Cleveland used me in two groups. In the Gospel Chimes, a quartet, I got to sing a lot. In the Cleveland Singers I played organ while Billy Preston played piano."

(Preston, who would hop back and forth across the gospel/secular line numerous times over the next two decades, later played piano for Ray Charles, the Rolling Stones, and the Beatles.)

It was in part through his association with Cleveland that Dixon got a contract with Savoy records—a contract that led to more than a dozen recordings, including a few gold albums and Grammy nominations.

His work with Cleveland also made Jessy a household name for the hundreds of thousands of Cleveland fans.

"And later, Leonard Chess called me," says Jessy. "I'm not sure how he heard of me, but he gave me a call and asked me to play on some secular sessions at the Chess studios."

Among the people Jessy recorded with was Willie Dixon (no relation), the Mississippi-born blues master who went north in 1937 and helped put the Chicago Blues on the map. A prolific composer whose compositions were recorded by hundreds of rock groups (Led Zeppelin recorded his "You Shook Me" and "I Can't Quit You, Baby" on their debut album, while the Doors featured his "Back Door Man" on their debut), Willie Dixon was not popular with many Christians who thought his music worldly and despondent. But Jessy wasn't worried. At least not yet.

I would play on Chess Records sessions, recording songs like Willie Dixon's "Wang Dang Doodle," and then go from there to choir rehearsal.

The whole time I was thinking, *I'm religious—a church boy, so I won't sing this secular stuff.* At the recording sessions they often didn't have the

words there anyway, just musicians laying down the rhythm tracks. I told myself that it was just notes. I didn't have any reservations about it because I wasn't singing it.

My pastor wasn't worried about it either. He said it was another way for me to grow.

His playing both secular and sacred music set the stage for Jessy to take a hard look at his own heart.

"Singing the Gospel" Versus "Believing the Gospel"

As Jessy started receiving more attention in both gospel and secular circles, he began to feel the tensions of a man torn between two lives.

Since I was doing both of these things, the lifestyles began to confuse me. And aside from me, I was seeing Gene Chandler, Jerry Butler, Sam Cooke, and the Staples Singers in the church and then out of it. And Aretha Franklin, who was recording her first album, was starting to go secular.

I realized I had to make a choice. More drugs were being presented to me. I was being offered marijuana and cocaine, and I was doing this and trying that. I was living a double life. I was playing for the church and the church people didn't know I was doing these other things. I just felt dirty inside.

Jessy sought spiritual counsel, but some of what he received didn't help much.

I would ask people if it was possible to be saved and still sin. They said, "The Lord understands." I knew there had to be more than this, because my mother and the other saved people I knew in Texas weren't doing this. I knew they didn't live two lives.

People in Chicago were trying to be too lenient with me. I presented such a wholesome image that nobody believed I could be leading another life. And some of the people were scared they might lose me, one pastor in particular because I was dating his niece. I would try to confess to pastors that I wasn't really saved, and they said, "Oh, you're here, you've grown up in the church. You're okay." I said, "I'm not."

It wasn't until late in 1971 that I got somewhere.

I went to a revival with my best friend, Ervin Adams. There was an altar call and Ervin and I looked at each other. I asked him if he was ready to go down, and he said no. He asked me if I was ready to go down, and I said no.

The next thing I remember was being in Dallas at a big convention. After the convention there was a big party with a lot of rock stars and a lot of drugs—pills, marijuana, everything. Suddenly I heard a voice tell me, "Pack your bags and leave." I went back to the hotel, packed, went to the airport, and flew to Chicago.

Things like that began to happen to me more and more, and I began to have more ambivalence about the life I was leading. Then, the next thing I knew, Ervin rang my doorbell and told me he had received the Lord. I almost passed out. I said to myself, *You mean I've been playing and singing in church all this time and never really listening to what anybody was saying?* I was jealous of him for months.

Ervin felt that if he had received the Lord, I should too. He just wouldn't take no for an answer. He witnessed to me until it was coming out of my ears. And I could see a real change in his life.

He asked me to go to church with him, and I thought if I went with him I could get rid of him. But he took me to a new converts' seminar with a guy talking about how to be saved. The night after he took me to church I came home and with some friends got as high as could be. I was really trying to blot out what I had heard the night before. I remember picking up a Bible and reading Romans 12 about presenting your body as a living sacrifice, and I said nobody can do that!

The next morning I was taking my car to be serviced, and I turned on the radio. There was a pastor talking—I think it must have been Kenneth Copeland. Ervin must have been in my car fooling with the radio, because I wouldn't have turned it to that station. But while I was listening my heart became open and I received the Lord while driving down the street.

"Have You Heard the NEW Jessy?"

Like a sculptor who had suddenly discovered how much help a hammer and chisels could be, now that Jessy knew the Jesus that appeared in so many of his songs he took to singing the gospel with a new zeal. One of the first things he did was to go through his entire repertoire,

getting rid of songs that weren't true to the gospel.

"I threw a lot of my material away," he says. "A lot of it was scripturally inaccurate, because before I knew Him I was totally blind.

"One song was 'Save a Seat for Me,' as if somebody can save you a seat in heaven! Another one was about what tomorrow would bring, while the Bible says to take no thought for tomorrow. The songs sounded great, but I couldn't do them anymore."

One of the first opportunities the new-and-improved, fired-up Jessy had to perform his new song list was at the 1971 Newport Jazz Festival, held at New York's Radio City Music Hall.

Jessy hadn't pushed and shoved his way onto the concert's bill. Again, someone had heard him and invited him to appear.

"One of the organizers had been a fan of mine," says Jessy. "He had seen me with James Cleveland and heard some of my Savoy albums."

Jessy nearly stole the show that night. He sang for twenty minutes, his allotted time, but the audience demanded four encores.

"I was a new Christian," says Jessy. "I was so anointed with the Holy Spirit that when I sang the people just went crazy."

Again, just as in San Antonio, somebody was to hear Jessy that night; and again, it would change his life.

In the audience was a well-known songwriter who was the "Tom" of the fifties group Tom and Jerry (remember the 1957 Top 50 hit, "Hey, Schoolgirl"?). Perhaps you might know him better as Simon in the sixties, seventies, and eighties group, Simon and Garfunkel.

No matter how you know him best, Paul Simon was in the audience. He listened as Jessy sang and watched as the crowd went wild.

Ever since Simon and Garfunkel had broken up in 1970, Simon had been looking for new musicians and singers for his upcoming concert tour. Within weeks, Simon's office had contacted Jessy, inviting him to travel with the popular singer/songwriter and offering him an attractive salary if he would accept. The call caught Jessy off guard.

"I really didn't know who Paul Simon was," said Jessy. "I wasn't into pop music. I had to have them send me all of his albums. Before they got to me I ran to the record store to see what he looked like. Then I said, 'Oh, this guy.' "

Now that he knew who Simon was, Jessy had to make a decision, and quick.

"I approached it as a way to witness," says Jessy, "because by that time I was thinking about winning the whole world for Jesus. But another factor was that Paul Simon had such integrity. His music was not anything anybody would be ashamed to be associated with."

Jessy made up his mind. He accepted Simon's offer, beginning an eight-year partnership that would take Jessy and his exciting brand of gospel music to audiences all around the world.

Rhymin' With Simon

Jessy's tours with Paul Simon, which began in 1972, were a unique combination of black gospel revival and Simon's catchy, quirky pop. Jessy, along with his band and the Jessy Dixon Singers, presented an unadulterated gospel message to thousands of pleasantly surprised listeners.

"Paul wouldn't let me be the opening act," says Jessy. "He would open the concerts himself, then he would bring me on to sing a few solos. He brought me on at such a highlight point of the concert that people were open to the gospel. Over the years, my portion of the concert grew longer and longer, and Paul said to go ahead and sing what I wanted."

Jessy's selections usually included a rousing version of Andrae Crouch's "Jesus Is the Answer," which wound up on Simon's 1974 album, *Paul Simon in Concert: Live Rhymin'*; "What Do You Call Him," a song confronting listeners with the person of Christ; "You Bring the Sun Out"; and "Operator."

Jessy and his singers also provided background for a number of Simon and Garfunkel hits, with Jessy singing Garfunkel's part to classics like "Bridge Over Troubled Water," "The Boxer," and others.

"My voice can get up there pretty high," says Jessy.

Adding to the gospel feel of the concerts were "Gone At Last" and "Loves Me Like a Rock," two Simon compositions that pay tribute to the black gospel idiom. And for many of the concerts, the grand finale was a duet by Jessy and Simon on the traditional hymn, "Amazing Grace." Jessy didn't realize then that all this was a breakthrough.

I think we added to the Simon concerts musically. But I also feel it was an excellent opportunity to share Jesus with these people. I felt so free; there was no opposition. While I was singing people would light their cigarette lighters, and the whole place would be lit up like a candlelight service.

I was a new Christian, and I didn't know I was pioneering anything. Pat Boone was the first Christian artist to tell me what I was doing was unusual. He said I wasn't being heckled and was being able to do what he and others hadn't been able to do. I hadn't realized that.

But when I became a Christian it wasn't like Dylan, who had been singing secular music and was now singing Christian music. I wasn't crossing over; it was reversed. I was a Christian singing some secular music, and I didn't think how unique that was.

Others, including writers for *Billboard* magazine, *Rolling Stone,* and newspapers from around the globe, *did* think about it, and were amazed. Sometimes, especially when Simon was having voice problems, these publications said that Dixon was the highlight of the show.

The *Los Angeles Times'* pop music critic Robert Hilburn commented on "the joyous Jessy Dixon Singers," writing: "It was the Dixons that really got things moving."

The *Chicago Tribune's* Lynn Van Matre praised Dixon and crew who, she said, "provided some of the evening's best moments."

"It wasn't until part way through the second half of the show, when Simon and crew were joined by the Chicago gospel group, the Jessy Dixon Singers, that things finally took off," wrote Van Matre, in an article headlined "Dixon Singers lend spark to Simon's simple show."

Didn't Jessy and his musicians encounter trials and temptations on the road?

"We had plenty of fellowship together," says Jessy. "We felt so protected by the Lord. Simon and his musicians respected us. They didn't even want to curse around us. They respected the fact that we were not just singing gospel music as an art form," he says, perhaps thinking back to earlier days. "They respected us as Christians."

Jessy's faith in and love for God showed in concert. At times audiences were won over by Dixon's electrifying presence and Spirit-inspired dancing more than by his singing. Such may have been the case during Rhymin' Simon's 1980 concert in Israel. Dixon sang "What Do You Call Him" to the largely Jewish audience. The response was best described by Rob Martin, writing in *Contemporary Christian Music* magazine:

Picture it, a black Christian from Chicago, full of Jesus, asking a Jewish audience in Israel by what name they called their Messiah, and the audience asking for more!

Dixon's stay in Israel also proved that Simon was as gracious off stage as on.

"When we got to Israel, Paul had a special car and a tour guide for us," says Jessy. "He said, 'I want Jessy to go to Jesus' tomb, and anyplace else that any Christian who ever went to Israel would go.' "

Even after Jessy and Simon parted professional ways in 1980, Simon continued to show his love and respect for the singer and his gospel. "He has called to ask me for prayer," says Jessy. "Paul believed in prayer, and he believes that if you are a Christian you are close to God.

"Paul is not sure, though, if he is close to God. Maybe the Lord is using me to reach Paul like he used Ervin to reach me."

Body Work

Jessy Dixon's life didn't begin on the day Paul Simon called him, and it didn't end when the concerts with Simon came to an end. Instead, he again turned his attention to singing for smaller secular audiences and, later, churches, and presenting his music and testimony to those who would listen.

Even while he was still associated with Simon, Jessy used his off-road time to perform secular college concerts, and he would use the opportunities to give the testimony that he wasn't able to share from a Simon concert stage.

I would sing my songs along with some of the Simon material, giving them my testimony as I went along. I would ask the people to meet me after the concert in the student union if they had questions or wanted to talk about the faith, and

usually twenty or thirty students would show up.

At about the same time I started doing some records for Light Records, and Andrae Crouch, who was on the label then, heard me. He said he had known me since childhood, but he didn't know I was saved until he had heard me in a concert in Chicago.

Andrae told me I had a ministry to the body of Christ, and that I should think and pray about that. I did, and I started getting more chances to play for churches.

I discovered that as I would give my testimony, people would give their hearts to the Lord. I felt that people were coming to hear me do more than sing. There are role models like Prince, but maybe I could be another type of role model who says, "I can sing, but listen to what else I do."

But he was still singing, and even writing. Jessy's 1982 Light album, *Satisfied*, which was recorded live at Calvary Chapel in Costa Mesa, California, demonstrated Jessy's talents in a live concert setting while showing that even a largely white Jesus Movement audience responded happily to his performance—a combination of black gospel, rhythm and blues, and ballads.

For eight years Jessy (at organ) and the Jessy Dixon Singers were a highlight of concerts by Paul (Rhymin') Simon.

Two of the ballads on *Satisfied* were Jessy's compositions. "Through the Blood" is a pretty and powerful song about Christ's cleansing power:

Through the blood, through the blood of Jesus Christ
We're triumphant and we reign victoriously
Living in a world of darkness
He came and brought the light
And it's shining bright for all the world to see
To my heart was the blood applied
At the cross where Jesus bled and died for me
It was there He bled and suffered, willingly He died
So that we could reign with Him eternally

"He Really Didn't Have to Die" is a beautiful and moving song about God's unmerited grace.

The Father gave His Son and the Son gave His life
To take away all the sins of the world
To everyone who would believe
To everyone who would receive
To every man and woman, boy and girl
He really didn't have to die
He really didn't have to die
He really didn't have to die, but He did
He loved humanity
So He died for you and me
He really didn't have to, but I'm glad He did

In 1983 Jessy moved to the Benson recording company for his next release, *Sanctuary*. But the singer, and numerous listeners, say that album failed to hit the mark.

"The album was laid back," says Jessy, "more laid back than I really am. The producers and I had different visions of what it should sound like."

But on Jessy's 1985 album, *Silent Partner*, the producer and the singer agreed readily about the sound they were after. The result is one of the best sounding albums of Jessy's long and impressive career.

Jessy and the Light Brigade

Silent Partner was produced by Dana Key, of DeGarmo & Key. The popular duo also helped write half the album's songs. Jessy was very pleased with the results:

I really like *Silent Partner*. It's music of the eighties, music for these times. It's the closest thing to me that I've ever done.

The partnership with DeGarmo & Key began in early 1985. We had meetings to see if we clicked as people and friends, to see if our hearts were going to blend together, to see if, theologically, we spoke the same language. And we did.

It's worked out really well. It's a natural match-up, because their music is rhythm-and-blues-influenced pop. They listened to Jimi Hendrix and Al Green and you can tell. They occasionally do "That's the Way God Planned It," an old Billy Preston song.

Musically and lyrically, *Silent Partner* presents Dixon at his best. "Celebrate the Lord," which opens the album, is an up-tempo number by John Elliott and Mark Baldwin that urges, "Let your joyful praises begin." "Face to Face" is a pretty and thoughtful DeGarmo & Key composition that shows the importance of faith in the midst of uncertainty.

"Radiate," a driving number, touches hearts while it sets feet to tapping. And the title song is about the "invisible security" God provides through angels.

"Destined to Win" is an encouraging and soul-stirring duet with Dana Key which reminds believers that they are surrounded by the infinite love and power of God, while the quiet and peaceful "My Heart Is His," a song of devotion and surrender, finds Jessy's voice at its deep and resonant best.

Jessy also took his music on the road with DeGarmo & Key for their ninety-city "Tour of the Light Brigade."

No, he's not showing any signs of sitting on his laurels or slowing down. As always, he sets his sights on the future.

"I would like to write more," he says. "I have been so busy with touring and traveling that I haven't been able to write as much as I would have liked to. But I won't be able to tour and sing like this forever."

That's okay, Jessy. You've given us more to listen to and draw courage from than you may realize. Thanks for singing your heart out.

Opposite page: Jessy teamed up with Degarmo & Key for the ninety-city "Tour of the Light Brigade" in 1985–86.

Chapter Four

LESLIE PHILLIPS

Leslie Phillips—in her life and her music—embraces many of the contradictions of being a Christian in these tumultuous times.

She is a contemporary woman: in the way she sounds, the way she looks, and the songs she writes. As comfortable in the quiet of her prayer closet as she is on the streets of her native Los Angeles, Phillips values both an intimacy with God and a sound knowledge of her own day and age.

And for her, music is more than music. It's not only a powerful way to fight evil and spiritual darkness, it is also, as she sings in her composition "Song in the Night," a metaphor for the miracle that Christ has done in the lives of all believers:

> *After midnight all is still*
> *The world sleeps without a sound*
> *Cold just cuts into your soul*
> *And you know death is all around*
> *As we gather on a hill*
> *In the dark someone starts a song*
> *Like an army we move out*
> *To fight the evil and the wrong*
>
> *(And like a) song in the night*
> *We'll sing our way through darkness*
> *We'll be true to the light*
> *And burn the gates of hell*

"I communicate through the vehicle of music," Leslie told Jane Pauley and the audience of NBC-TV's "Today" show.

The song in the night
Will bring life to those who hear it
And Jesus has given us
A song in the night

Not only can Christians act as songs in this long night of the world, but Christian songs can serve as fiery darts against ignorance and evil. In fact, Leslie Phillips is firmly convinced that music can be more than music, and she has thought so since she was ten years old. It was then that she had an encounter with music that led directly to an encounter with God.

My brother Bob had become a Christian in junior high school, and in 1972 he took me to hear *Come Together*, a musical written by Jimmy and Carol Owens.

I was young, but already a lot of things were at war for my soul. I was being witnessed to by a Mormon girl, and I was starting to dabble in the occult. I think this happens to kids today in so many ways. So for me, the musical came at an important time in my life. And I don't really know why, but I cried through the whole thing. Suddenly I knew that whatever life was all about, this was it—being a Christian.

That musical was the first time I had heard modern music and songs about Christianity, and I realized that Jesus was for everybody—young or old. He transcends culture, and He transcends the distinctions between old and new, mind and heart.

But contemporary Christian music continued to be important to me, not only in my salvation but as I grew in the Lord. The role models of people in Christian music were so important to me.

When we were growing up, my girl friends and I used to say we would like to be the kind of girls Randy Stonehill would like—somebody who loves God, is crazy, is himself, and is really sensitive to what the Lord is doing in his life.

And it wasn't just Randy—with whom I have now had the opportunity to tour for six months—but other people were good role models for me, people like Keith Green, the Second Chapter of Acts, and others had an influence in my life.

Great! So all we have to do is listen to Christian music and everything will be all right, right?
Wrong.

As Leslie says,

Music isn't everything. Music is an important thing and people are attracted to the music, but for some people the music becomes too important at the expense of everything else.

People shouldn't make Christian music their entire spiritual diet—that would be like eating candy all the time. It would be wrong for somebody to think they could survive on music and get by without fellowshipping, studying the Bible, and spending time alone with the Lord.

Christian music definitely has its purpose—to encourage people and reach people. I think of a band like Stryper that is doing something in heavy metal music. They are playing a vital role in communicating to people who would never listen to Christian music from anybody else.

That makes me think of King David whaling on his harp. I wonder if he were here today what instrument he would use.

Real Music for Real People

It may be a while before we can talk to David and ask him for his perspective on modern instrumentation. And while we're at it, we can ask him how he liked the way Leslie used his words for her version of Psalm 55.

Most of the time, though, she isn't using King David's words or anybody else's words on her albums. She writes just about everything herself—all but four of the thirty songs on her first three albums.

And that's okay. Her songs are good. They're real.

She doesn't paint some inspirational postcard-perfect picture of the way she wishes everything was. She doesn't look through rose-colored glasses with *Jesus Loves You* inscribed on the frames. No, she tells us about life. Real life, with all the struggles, challenges, and failures that go together to make up our earthly existence.

Most of her songs bear unmistakable clues that they weren't ground out in five minutes of idle reflection but were byproducts of actual experiences in somebody's life. And usually that life was Leslie's.

I wasn't raised in a Christian home, and I think that because of that I never had Christianity stuffed down my throat. I really had to figure it out on my own, and that was good. In my walk with the Lord I have had to ask a lot of questions.

In my music I try to be real honest about the things I am going through. There are times I am being disciplined and I wonder, *Lord, why are things so crazy and why do I feel this way?*

Her honesty can be seen in the first song she recorded, "Bring Me Through," which was written at a time of personal struggle. The song appeared on a 1981 Maranatha! Music sampler album called *Back to the Rock,* as well as her own 1983 debut album:

I've been in the basement
Groping for the light
But it just goes to show me
That I walk by faith and not by sight
But now I feel the walls are closing in
The dark is blacker than it's ever been . . . Lord

Deep inside I'm bleeding
With nothing to ease the pain
Aching memories beating
Like a cold, pulsating rain
The more I try to fight
The more I fail
Condemnation's got me by the tail . . . Lord

You've gotta bring me through
'cuz there's nothing more I can do
You've gotta bring me through
I'm leaving it up to You

Two things were happening to me when I wrote that. First, I was going through the loss of a best friend. Second, I was working for a man who got deep into prophecy and started getting strange ideas, one of which was that his wife was going to die and I was going to take her place.

I really wanted to be open to the Holy Spirit and the gifts of the Spirit. I wanted not to despise prophecy, but test it. God was letting me get a little disillusioned with people for the first time. And it hurt.

But pain is something we all feel. It's universal, whether we lose a pet or lose a loved one. There are different levels of pain, and I write about those times because they are a very real part of life.

Another sad fact of life is failure, and Leslie writes about her failures—and God's help—in a number of songs. Submitted as evidence: two songs from *Black and White in a Grey World.*

"When the World Is New" is a slow, pretty ballad that opens with a mournful verse about human faithlessness but closes with a glowing declaration of God's faithfulness.

I get so tired of myself
Jaded by shame
No wonder people turn away
When I give You such a bad name
But it's so nice to know

When the world is new
I will be like
Be like You

"Your Kindness," another beautiful ballad, describes the feelings of guilt and imminent condemnation that are eased by God's infinite grace.

Waiting for angry words to sear my soul
Knowing I don't deserve another chance
Suddenly the kindest words I've ever heard
Come flooding from God's heart

It's Your kindness that leads us
To repentance Oh Lord
Knowing that You love us
No matter what we do
Makes us want to love You too

Leslie talks about how she came to write it:

"Your Kindness" was written after I broke off an engagement with a man I had been dating for four years. I did not handle it very well. I had blown it and really made a mess of the whole thing. I was ready to get it from God, and thought I had better hide. But when I really did face the Lord in quiet time I felt His incredible grace. God loves us even if we hurt Him.

It's important for me to communicate in my music the fact that I make mistakes and fail. I remember sitting in the audience watching Christian performers and thinking they must have it all together. I thought they were beautiful people, and wondered how I could ever be like that.

So one of the things I really determined to do was show my human side, my failures in everyday life so my listeners won't feel like I did or won't feel like they can't get close to the Lord because they are this way or that way.

"Gina," a song from *Beyond Saturday Night*, tells the story of another failure—this one fatal.

"Gina" is a true story about a girl friend of mine in high school. She was having family problems, and in her junior or senior year of high school she dropped out. I thought about calling her and spending some time with her, but I didn't because I was busy.

The next thing I knew I read in the paper that she had died in a car accident. This song talks about the consequences of my actions. Not that God doesn't forgive me, but that sometimes the damage is permanent.

Beauty and the Beast

Leslie portrays not only the hard things in life, but the good things as well. Some of her songs are full and joyous testimonies to the beauty of life and the blessings of God.

"Strength of My Life" ("Every day I look to You to be the strength of my life") and "By My Spirit" ("Not by might, not by power / But by my Spirit says the Lord"), two ballads from *Dancing With Danger*, are pretty, melodic songs that praise God for His goodness. They are hardly rock numbers and it isn't difficult to imagine Sandi Patti or Larnelle Harris singing them at a Billy Graham rally.

"You're My Lord," a gentle, moving praise number, and "You're the Same," an upbeat song about God's constancy in the face of our fickleness, both from *Black and White*, show that there's room in Leslie's heart and music for the joy of the Lord.

Leslie's voice covers all the bases. She can coo like a dove or scream like a banshee, as the material dictates. And she is also adept at describing the agents on the other side of this cosmic battle called life. Satan, his cohorts, and his ploys appear on Leslie's *Dancing With Danger* album.

"Dancing With Danger" is a catchy rock number that paints a clear picture of those who put their faith on hold and dabble with sin:

Raised with a Bible in your hand
You met your parents' strict demands
But now that sweet religious child
Is like a hurricane gone wild

And you're dancing
Dancing with danger
Lies from a stranger
Waltz inside your head
You've got your back to
The One who really loves you
But you can't stop because
You can't see what's ahead

You've danced yourself out on a ledge
Your dreams are falling off the edge

God never wanted it that way
He wants to shake your fears away

"Traveling around so much, I see a lot of kids who were brought up in the church or who have been Christians for a while," she says. "And a lot of us are like that. We think, *Well, I wonder what I can get away with? Let's lay back for a while and have some fun.*

"But sometimes we really don't realize what we're doing or see how serious things are. Sin is fun for a season, but we don't really realize what a backlash there is and how serious things can get."

The song's lyrics drive home Leslie's point, but just as important is the hard-driving rock arrangement by guitarist Dann Huff which gives the song its impact. As Leslie explains,

I like the fact that I could write it in a rock vein. A lot of times people who aren't Christians use rock music for rebellion. When they feel like rebelling they'll crank up a hot rock song. I thought that by doing a song like this I could counteract these feelings, redirect them, and rebel against rebellion.

Sometimes rock is a beautiful art form that can give a punch to a song that nothing else can—that can give it drama, that can drive home a point where a lilting ballad is not going to do it. For Christians, rock music can express our passion for the Lord—our will for good, not bad.

Instead of people saying, "Hey, let's go out and let's party," I wanted to give them a song that said, "Watch out, you can hurt yourselves."

In "I Won't Let it Come Between Us," another rock number arranged by Huff, Leslie provides a description of the beauty of evil that is so realistic the listener almost feels he can reach out and touch it.

You know wrong can sure look good sometimes
And it's caught my eye just like a jewel that shines
It calls to me like one of my old friends
But it's trying to tear my heart from Yours in the end

A world of pleasure laying at my feet
The wine of recklessness can taste so sweet
But nothing stirs my soul like knowing You
Yet evil's foot is in the door and it's coming through

The rebel in me's hungry to be wild
And I listen to her like a foolish child
Driven by desires in the wind
I find I'm eye to eye with sin again

But I won't let it, no I won't let it
No I won't let it come between us
I just won't let it, no I won't let it
No I won't let it come between us
Because, Lord, Your love's too precious to me now

I was told in church that evil was terrible and awful, which it is. But the seductive beauty of evil was never addressed. In youth group I heard that evil could never be fun or appealing.

But the Bible also says that Satan is a beautiful, beautiful angel who comes to us as an angel of light. He really puts on a good face.

In this song I'm saying something that a lot of people won't openly admit—that evil can be fun. People are afraid to look at that side of it, but we need to. It's like C. S. Lewis's *Screwtape Letters*, which shows how Satan tries to make evil fun.

Leslie's albums of slice-of-life songs have sold well—nearly a quarter million's worth. She is thankful, even vindicated.

I am surprised at my success. I was signed at a time when Word Records was cutting its artists roster, and the fact that people like my music proves something I have felt for a long time—that people have a need for music that is real, that talks about the things they go through, the things they don't understand.

I haven't done a whole album of Scripture songs, although they're important. I want to do songs that talk about modern life and being a Christian in the modern world.

Christian music has improved in the last decade, but I don't know if songwriting has improved. There are still a lot of insincere lyrics in Christian music. I hope people are open to God and are letting Him do things in their hearts so they can write about them.

Being in music is a weighty responsibility. But our main job is just to be ourselves, follow Him, and be comfortable with what we do for Him. My approach is to be very honest. I'm not trying to be somebody who has all the answers.

Life in Full Color

Where does Leslie get the inspiration to create both rockers and ballads? How can she write songs that display an understanding of both God and evil? And why did a St. Petersburg newspaper critic, who seemed to be scrambling for comparisons, say this about her concert performance: "She sings like Pat Benatar, dances like Sheila E., and gives the gospel like Amy Grant"?

Leslie credits her church.

I'm really grateful for the Church on the Way in Van Nuys. Jack Hayford, the pastor there, presents a very balanced view of the Christian faith. I've been exposed to a lot of mature Christian

behind, and that was a very valid ministry for him. Others focus on praise and worship music. I'm supposed to express all these facets.

I would hope that I could attract people who never listen to anything else but praise music. Maybe in their lives they are not dealing with some basic, down-to-earth issues. I hope they would come to listen to this piece of life.

For the people who love rock music and who are into the nitty-gritty, earthy things, I would hope some of the softer songs make a place in

people there who live balanced Christian lives. It's taught me a lot.

There are a lot of different aspects of God. There is the angry God of the Israelites in a cloud of smoke and fire, and there is the loving Jesus, who became a servant and sat down and washed the feet of the disciples, which were probably pretty grimy back in those days.

There are different facets to the Lord. Keith Green felt he was supposed to kick people in the

their hearts. There's a value to praise and worship, to being soft and open before the Lord. And having that personal relationship with Him is very important.

I don't want to be labeled as one particular thing. Some people think I'm a blonde from California, an airhead, a female rock and roller who can't write praise songs. I want to be different and let people know that praising God is part of my life and should be part of theirs too.

But Leslie's songs don't stay within the confines of the church and "the world as Christians see it." The song "The More I Know You," from *Black and White,* finds her taking a unique view of evangelism, balancing the urgency of saving the lost with the need to show them a personal love:

You're not just a notch in my belt
Hunted by religious ego
A conquest of the narrow-minded blind
Your smile is the pulse of my heartbeat
I care what you do with your soul
There's no one like you
You're a rare and precious find

The more I know you
The more I want you to know

And *Dancing With Danger's* "Light of Love" finds her tackling the difficult subject of premarital sex:

I don't want to love you
At least not the way you're thinking

I don't want to climb the stairs up to your room
'cuz up there in the darkness
The love that we'd reach for
Would disappear at dawn with the fading moon

And in the light of love
You'll see how long it takes for love to be
In the light of love
I'll wait to have you and you'll wait to have me

She had expected more negative reaction to that song.

It would have been a lot safer to ignore the whole issue of sex, but surprisingly, I have not received one negative letter or call about the song. What this shows me is that society has become so bad, our views on sex have become so warped, and we are bombarded by so much evil that people are glad I brought it up. It seems that a lot of people are hungry for someone to say something healthy about sex.

But it was a hard song to write, because I didn't

want to say you should not have sex and here are five biblical reasons why. I wanted to write this from the perspective that this is something that I have to deal with. It is often a hard decision, but I have to stand up for righteousness.

God's Not Through With Her Yet

The future looks bright for Leslie Phillips, who at twenty-four is seeing her career take off. But she isn't the type to get caught up in it all. For her, all is to know God.

I remember watching a good friend of mine who is involved with network television. He "has everything," but watching his life was so frustrating—seeing how much he was missing, rationalizing his actions, saying that nothing matters and that there are no values or absolutes.

How awful life becomes without values. How warped and colorless. All the colors run together into a mudlike life. But Jesus brings the colors into crystal clarity. We need answers and absolutes, and it's so comforting to know that they are really there.

As you might suspect, she wrote a song about it, the title song from *Black and White in a Grey World*:

Ooh, I feel so out of place
Like I've landed on the moon
You can see it in my face
I don't mind being different
'Cuz I'm different for the truth
And I'm black and white in a grey world

Chapter Five

MICHAEL OMARTIAN

Michael Omartian's name may not be a household word, at least not in most households. But whether they know it or not, people in just about every home in the land have heard some of the music this talented and hard-working artist has helped create.

For example, ever heard of Rod Stewart? How about Christopher Cross or Donna Summer? Ever tapped your toes to Steely Dan, hummed along with Loggins & Messina, boogied down with Al Jarreau, been bluesy with Boz Scaggs, or been countrified by Dolly Parton?

If so, you've probably heard the music of Michael Omartian.

On the gospel side (where he makes less than half the money, but gives just as much time and attention), Omartian has worked with Debby Boone, the Imperials, Benny Hester, and others. And while you may not have been a big fan of Vapour Trails, Gatorcreek, or Ted Neely (remember the guy who played Christ in *Jesus Christ Superstar*, and whose forte was acting, not singing?), Michael was there too.

Through his work on keyboards and percussion, his writing and arranging, and his skill as a producer, Michael Omartian has been helping these artists make their music sound bigger and better.

As a committed Christian making music in Los Angeles, the place Joni Mitchell called "the city of the fallen angels," Omartian has earned a solid reputation for honesty, integrity, and the ability to make hits. He has also earned the respect of both those who share his faith and those for whom Christianity is the ancient-sounding antithesis of everything that is hip, sexy, and lucrative.

Along the way he has made some great music and shown everyone who has eyes to see that following Jesus is not only a necessity, it is also life-enriching.

Mr. Hit

When Michael Omartian came to Los Angeles in 1969, he brought with him his faith in God; his long-developing skills on piano and percussion; and a love for all types of music, from the Beatles to Bach to Brubeck.

"I started classical piano lessons at age four, took up drums at five, and studied jazz piano in junior high," says Michael. "It's the melding together of jazz, classical, and—in the later years—rock that made me whatever I am now musically."

Laughing, he adds, "I'm still trying to figure that out!"

Along with his unmistakable talent, Michael brought an amazingly strong drive to succeed. But his zeal and determination didn't spring from the desire to get filthy rich; rather they were the consequences of an extremely demanding mother.

"All my life she demanded nothing less than perfection," he says. "If I got a *B* on my report card she would ask why I didn't get an *A*. If I got an *A* she would ask why my jacket had a stain on it."

But Michael tried to bury the ghosts of his childhood and concentrated, instead, on his career.

In 1970, after a number of small jobs and music industry contacts, he became involved with two then relatively unheard-of musicians—Kenny Loggins and Jim Messina. "That was one of my first experiences playing in L.A.," remembers Michael.

> Loggins and Messina got together to form a duo and Loggins got me involved. Then the three of us worked on our songs and recruited other players. We recorded *Sittin' In*, which came out in 1971, and after the record did well they wanted to take this thing on the road for a tour.
>
> But by that time—through other associations and work—people were listening to what I was playing and they wanted me to play on their records. I was becoming very involved in session work. And I had to take a look at the economics of it. Was I going to stay here in town and play for a lot of people or would I go on the road with a brand-new band?

Loggins and Messina went on the road without Michael (although he also played on 1972's *Loggins and Messina* and 1973's *Full Sail*), and as the band's road turned gold farther on, Michael began to discover the joys of playing and arranging.

He played keyboards and helped with arrangements on many early-seventies releases: Billy Joel's 1973 debut *Piano Man*, Ted Neely's 1974 *A. D.*, and Steely Dan's *Pretzel Logic* (1974) and *Katy Lied* (1975). By 1975 he had become involved in production work as well.

> I started as a keyboard player, but wound up arranging. That is basically taking what the artist is doing and converting it to all the instruments. If the artist sits there and strums the song on his guitar or just sings it, you have to work out the parts and assign them to musicians. You take the song as far as it will go musically.
>
> But after that, I figured I needed to be a producer too. An arranger doesn't have anything to do with picking the song itself, or mixing what's recorded, or having a relationship with the record company's promotion department; while a producer, on the other hand, is responsible for overseeing the whole project.
>
> It's like a movie producer who goes out and gets the script, hires the director, etc. And I'm a songwriter too, so I'll wind up writing things with the artist.

One of Michael's first opportunities to act as arranger and producer came in 1975 with a musical group called Rhythm Heritage. The group had a number 1 hit in February of 1976 with Michael's arrangement of a song from a popular TV show: "The Theme From S. W. A. T."

According to Michael:

> This was back before "Miami Vice" and MTV. At that time people in the movie and television industry didn't know people in the music business. Somebody came up with a brilliant idea, that a show could go a little further with some exposure on Top-40 radio. We decided to do the theme from "S. W. A. T." and got a number 1 record.
>
> There was a group of studio musicians: Scotty Edwards on bass, Ed Greene on drums, Jay Graydon on guitar, Victor Feldman on percussion, and me. You get used to playing with each other, and those guys were so proficient at what they did you didn't have to waste time waiting for somebody to rise to the occasion. They could play anything, which is what the whole concept of studio players was.

The "S. W. A. T." theme appeared on a 1976 album called *Disco-Fied*, which also featured "Baretta's Theme," "Three Days of the Condor," and two tunes co-written by

Omartian. (The cover of the album featured the weird-est-looking shoe ever known to woman—a fuzz-covered, nine-inch platform atrocity. But the music was good!)

It wasn't exactly art for art's sake, but Omartian, now a staff producer at ABC Records, was getting a reputation as a hit maker. Rhythm Heritage recorded two later albums. "We tried a couple of new things and tried to stretch out a little," says Michael. "We tried to become an entity that wasn't dependent on TV and movie themes, but it didn't work. We found out that's what the connection with the public was."

To Live and Love in L. A.

Meanwhile, Michael and his wife, Stormie, were showing that there was more to life in L. A. than music, money, and madness. Life could be lived in a loving relationship to people and God, and music could reflect both art and ministry.

In 1974, one year after they had been married, Michael and Stormie worked together on their first album, *White Horse*, released on ABC records. Their partnership set the pattern for four later albums together: Michael wrote the music and Stormie wrote the lyrics. But, as Michael explains, public response to that first album was not overwhelming:

I went to the people at ABC and said I would really like to do a record. They were all gung ho, so they said go ahead and do it.

When they got the tapes they were surprised. It was very progressive, even by the standards of secular music at the time, and they were all excited about the music end of it. But they couldn't figure out what the heck was going on lyrically, and that kind of threw them.

ABC was distributing Word Records at that time, and when Word got wind of this thing, they asked if they could buy it out. So Word brought out *White Horse*, and suddenly it was put in Christian stores. And still people couldn't figure out what we were talking about.

Folks at ABC didn't grasp Stormie's lyrics, and gospel music buyers couldn't understand Michael's music. But *White Horse* remains one of the best, most professionally produced Christian records around.

Side one opened up with "Jeremiah," a rollicking song that pointed the finger at sin and unbelief.

Jeremiah, how your people cry.
"What's the answer. Don't let it change
the way we live or die."

55

No matter where you run,
You've got to pay for what you've done.

The song's next two verses related the prophecies of Obadiah and Zephaniah to modern times. Verse four returned to Jeremiah:

Jeremiah, how great your pain must be.
To have the answer, and yet the people still refuse to see.
Let there be no doubt,
There is only one way out.

Following each verse was the chorus:

I could set you free,
But you must turn back to me.

White Horse also included "Take Me Down," a song about baptism:

Round and round in that cistern altar.
Time goes down in the flowing water.
The past is washed away like weeping ashes.
Lift your hands as it passes.

"Silver Fish" was about growing in the faith.

Lord, I'm getting stronger.
Feeling it every day.
Worn-out reins and nameless chains,
Begin to fall away.

While "Fat City," sang about love, not lust:

Fat City,
I could be livin' in.
In Fat City, I could be sittin' real pretty.
But it wouldn't mean a thing without you.

I could build me a mansion with a solid gold fence,
But if you weren't around it wouldn't make much sense.
I could own a private plane, and a sailboat in Maine,
A tropical island and a narrow gauge train.
But if I didn't have you I could never stay sane.
No, I couldn't stay sane without you.

Both sacred and secular listeners may have missed the album's point, but it still stands as one of the most stunning musical performances on a Christian album.

Some musicians I know, like Jeff Porcaro of Toto and others, say they still pull that thing out

and listen to it. It was a musicians' kind of album. *White Horse* got a tremendous reception, but it didn't sell anything.

But I feel it was important for me to do that album. I didn't feel I was in the music business by accident. I felt I was supposed to say something. We wanted to be careful and didn't want to offend anyone, but we did want to get our faith across."

After *White Horse*, Michael and Stormie teamed up on *Adam Again*, which was done for Word's Myrrh label in 1976.

As with *White Horse*, *Adam Again* featured Stormie's lyrics, Michael's music and arrangements, and some of the best studio musicians Los Angeles had to offer. The album was a bit more accessible, and songs like "Whachersign," a satirical look at astrology ("I think I fell in love with you just a moment ago / But how can I be sure unless the stars tell me so"), seemed to guarantee greater popular acceptance. But still, *Adam Again* seemed to be going over the heads and right past the ears of most Christian music buyers. As Michael explains:

Until very recent times, the type of contemporary Christian music that has been most successful has been music bordering on easy listening.

We didn't really worry about sales. We never looked at our Christian records as a moneymaking proposition, because we're doing fine on the other end. Our motives were never to sell records. But we were getting pressure from the record company to do something they could get on Christian radio. So we tried a different approach for our next album.

Mr. and Ms. Past Meet Mr. Trash Man in the Office of Dr. Jesus

The next album, 1978's *Seasons of the Soul*, listed both Michael and Stormie Omartian as the album's artists. This was not another one of Michael's solo projects, and Stormie now did lead vocals on a number of songs. The album was a true collaboration.

Musically, Stormie and I are at opposite ends of the spectrum. She's not exactly a rock and roll singer, where I'm more inclined toward a heavier feel. And I never considered myself a singer anyway, so the louder it was and the more aggressive it sounded the more I could cover up what I was

Michael and Stormie have been making beautiful music together since their marriage in 1973.

doing. So in order to accommodate Stormie's and my tastes, we had to bring it to someplace in the middle. That was what we started doing on *Seasons of the Soul.*

But the music was not the only thing that was different on the new album. The lyrics became less abstract and more personal. Part of the personal touch in some of the songs came from the fact that the songs were coming from the deep and painful experiences both Michael and Stormie were going through.

Stormie, too, had had a rough childhood. Her mother was abusive, leaving emotional scars that lasted long into her adult life. Michael, likewise, continued to be haunted by the anxiety and depression that had led to his emotional breakdown in 1965.

As the couple received counseling and support at Church on the Way in Van Nuys, themes of healing from deep-seated hurts and growing in the grace of God began to surface more frequently on their records. "Ms. Past," the opening cut on *Seasons of the Soul,* was a declaration of spiritual war on the Old Man—and Woman:

> Ms. Past, she's such a wicked lady.
> Ms. Past, she's always there a waiting.
> She's the Devil's favorite tool,
> She'll play you for a fool,
> She'll cry until she rules.

> Don't look,
> Don't look back just let her go.
> Lately,
> All she's done is lay you low.

> Ms. Past, she'll always try to feed you.
> Ms. Past, she'll say He never freed you.
> Don't fall for her disguise,
> And look back in her eyes,
> She wants you paralyzed by all she knows.

"Travel on With Me" sang about "Sailin' on a sea called Compromise."

> Well, I learned to live the way that He wanted me to.
> I could see that He was boss.
> And anything I tried outside of His will,
> Would come to be a total loss.

Perhaps feeling the criticism of other Christians who wondered why Michael and Stormie were still dealing with the pain from their pasts, Stormie wrote the words to "Where I Been," which Michael belted out:

> I may not be as far along as you,
> But I started way behind.
> While you were making choices,
> I was trying to survive . . .

> If you think compared with you,
> I don't hold up as well.
> Well, Jesus had a lot to do,
> When He brought me back from Hell.

The Builder, Michael and Stormie's 1980 collaboration, contained two songs about Christ's power to heal the hurts of the past. One was "Mr. Trash Man."

> Oh, Mr. Trash Man,
> I'm glad you came today.
> I've got a selection
> Of things I'm throwing away.

> See Mr. Trash Man,
> I just cleaned out my heart.
> Don't know if it's over,
> But at least it's a start.

> Jesus said if I would come to Him,
> He'd take my past and I could start all over again
> Start again.

Another was "Dr. Jesus."

> Dr. Jesus it hurts so bad right here,
> Would you be so kind
> To check here deep inside my heart
> And just below my mind.
> Yes, I've had this pain for quite a while,
> A lifetime I believe.
> I've tried everything I know of
> And it never seems to leave.
> I've heard you're the only specialist
> Who's ever had the cure.
> The others only cover up
> A wound that's always there.
> You come highly recommended,
> In fact millions of people say
> If you want to be saved from death and all
> You've got the only way.

In a 1983 concert appearance with Second Chapter of Acts at Church on the Way (later made into a Sparrow Records two-disc album, *Together Live*) both Stormie and Michael testified to the continuation of the Lord's healing love and power in their lives.

"Michael and I are good examples of the restorative power of Jesus working in broken lives," said Stormie.

Faith Under Pressure

Michael continued to improve on his knack for making hits. He added his keyboard skills to albums by Al Jarreau, co-writing the infectious "Boogie Down" with the jazz singer for his 1983 *Jarreau* album.

In 1977, Michael played piano on "Aja," the beautiful title track from the popular and critically acclaimed album by Steely Dan. "Those guys were meticulous beyond reason," he says about the band's notorious habit of trying to make perfect records, "but at the same time it was very enjoyable. We would stretch and do things you never thought you could do."

Among their accomplishments: recording "Aja" live in one take.

Michael also improved his skills as a producer. The proof of that came in 1980 when Michael produced *Christopher Cross*, the debut album by the Austin, Texas, singer which landed in the Top 10 and yielded the single "Ride Like the Wind" which went to number 1.

That album went on to win Omartian a Grammy Award and eventually sold 9 million copies worldwide, which was good. The bad part was when Cross's second album sold only a paltry 3.5 million.

As Michael explains:

> When you have such an incredible success the first time, no matter what you do the second time it's very difficult to duplicate that. Michael Jackson will never be able to make another record that will sell 30 million copies.
>
> But there are new pressures on you when you have had a successful album. When you give the listeners more of the same, they hang you up against the wall. If you do something different, they ask you why you did something different.

For all the troubles success brought, it also brought benefits. For one, Michael was able to afford a studio in his house—something that saved money in the production of Michael and Stormie's albums, as well as recordings by other Christian artists.

"Let me give you an example," he says. "We recorded Christopher Cross's third album, *Every Turn of the World*, for about three hundred fifty thousand dollars. Debby Boone's *Choose Life* cost eighty thousand. I did most of the work at the house and didn't charge anything for studio time, which is up around two hundred dollars an hour at most places."

Another benefit of Cross's success was that Michael was able to leave Warner Brothers, where he had been working as a staff producer since 1977, and set up shop as Michael Omartian Productions.

But success was also testing Michael's faith. The first test came in 1977 with a song Michael coproduced. The song, "Undercover Angel," by Alan O'Day, went to number 1 in July of 1977, but the song's sexual innuendo caused it to be banned by some radio stations.

Understandably, some Christians raised questions about Michael's involvement in the project, and Michael says they were right to.

> They should have raised questions. I said back then it was a giant mistake I should never make again. I was so into music at the time that the Lord had to teach me that I just couldn't focus on what I liked about the music. I had to step back and listen to what the person was saying.
>
> It was a matter of taking responsibility and listening to what was being said, and I'm glad that happened before I became a solo producer because I really needed to understand that whole idea.

Another challenge came later on when Michael wound up in the studio with Seals & Crofts.

"At one point they sat me down and started giving me their whole Baha'i faith trip," says Michael. "I listened to what they said, and told them quite honestly that I didn't understand what they were talking about. Then I told them I believed in Jesus Christ and that He was my personal Savior, and they almost fell off their stools."

But the biggest challenge in Michael's professional life thus far came when he was asked to produce controversial rocker Rod Stewart's 1984 *Camouflage* album.

> I usually seek God's guidance about whether I should do a particular project, but I had to debate this one harder because of all the ramifications of the thing—because of the built-in problems people would have with what I felt Stewart represented.
>
> So my wife and I and two other people held a three-day fast about it, and after the time was over I made my decision to produce the album before I asked the other people their feelings. That was wrong of me. It was not being obedient to God by not seeking counsel. That was my fault. I'm not saying that God would have said no to the project, but it was the wrong way for me to approach it.

After that, the album went very smoothly. In fact there were two Christians in Rod's band who drew strength from our conversations and our time together. I encouraged them toward getting back to church and reading their Bibles and praying.

> And Rod and I had many opportunities throughout the project to talk about the Lord. The first day in the studio he was reading Pat Boone's testimony book, and later on he was reading books by Robert Schuller.

Things continued to go smoothly; Michael even wrote two songs with Stewart—"Trouble" and the album's title cut, "Camouflage." But, according to Michael, problems developed as Stewart was recording the last of the album's songs, a rocker that came to be called "Bad for You."

> The song was still being put together. There wasn't a title, and there weren't lyrics, and this was five and a half months into the project.
>
> Fifteen years ago nobody would present a song that wasn't finished, but today you're talking about 50 percent of an album being stuff that isn't finished at the time you begin. People sit down with their drum machines and synthesizers and work out a groove and worry about the lyrics later.
>
> Well, he started singing these lyrics and I said "What in the world is this?" I couldn't believe it. I asked him if he was going to change it. He said no. I said, "I'm going to have to do something about this. I need to put a disclaimer on there."

The disclaimer was simple and direct and was printed on the album's liner: "Please note: The song 'Bad for You' does not represent the views of Michael Omartian, a born-again Christian."

Both secular and religious publications made a big deal of the disagreement. Apparently accounts of the incident were wildly exaggerated. There was no yelling, screaming, or backstabbing.

Stewart told *Billboard* magazine his feelings:

> There was one time he wanted to change the lyrics in a song because he's a born-again Christian. But, generally speaking, I would love to work with him again, even though we did have a few punch-ups.

In fact, Michael says their parting was quite amicable, "At the end of the project, he said he really respected me for my beliefs and for what I did, but that he had to do what he had to do. I said that's okay."

And after all, Stewart had reason to be happy. Michael brought the album in for a cost of around three hundred twenty thousand dollars while more than a million had reportedly been spent on Stewart's previous album, *Foolish Behaviour*.

Also, "Infatuation," the album's opening cut, captured radio airplay during the summer of 1984, propelling the album to healthy sales.

Isn't it dangerous—even professional suicide—for a self-confessed "born-again Christian" to go around telling people what he is about and—what's more—making radical decisions on the basis of that faith?

Michael responds:

Something like that disclaimer can't help but cause ripples. You're dealing with an industry that is basically not godly and doesn't want to have anything to do with godliness. So consequently I was sticking my neck out.

I could have taken the advice of a lot of people who said to forget it—it would die or something. I just didn't feel right about it. I battled with it. I would go to bed at night thinking this would be the end of it for me.

But then I realized I'm not serving these people—I'm serving God, so I have to do what He tells me to do. I believe that one of the reasons I'm in the music business is to stick my neck out—to represent the antithesis of all I see going on all the time.

I'm not alone. There's other people out here doing the same thing. It's scary, but I feel I have a responsibility to God.

At one point Sheena Easton asked me to do some records for her. I thought, man, that would be great. It didn't work out, but who knew that she was going to record "Sugar Walls"?

There's no way to know when somebody will basically say, "Okay, I'll sell out," given the pressures on people today for what it takes to become successful. But you don't have to go along with it.

One Song Is Not Enough

What's next for Michael and Stormie?

"We probably won't be doing any records for a while," says Michael. "We had a child, and God was really calling Stormie to books. She's working on *Stormie—Story of God's Restoration*, about the abuse she suffered as a child and the healing she has received from God [to be published in the summer of 1986].

"And unless you live with someone who writes you can't really appreciate how much time it takes. So I don't just function as a musician or producer. I try as much as possible to help her out around here while she's working on her book. We try to help each other out."

As for Michael, look for the hits to continue.

You know, the same presidents of record companies who call me and tell me I shouldn't have put the disclaimer on the Stewart album call me up the next week and ask me to produce somebody for them.

Or take what happened with Peter Cetera, the former lead singer for Chicago. He came to talk to me about me producing his solo album, and he wanted to know what this born-again Christian stuff was all about. I explained my faith to him, and he said, "I don't know if I believe all that, but at least I know I can trust you and work with you."

Don't look for Michael to shed his faith. Rather, look for more hits from his Studio City offices.

"I don't see how a non-Christian can make it in this business," he says. "The temporary euphoria you get out of having a Top 10 hit will never make it in the long run because you're not going to have that forever. You're going to have to draw on something deeper."

Aside from all the hits, Michael may have a musical surprise or two up his sleeves. One is his newest recording, released in Christian stores on the Meadowlark label and distributed to mainstream stores by Capitol. "I have about forty minutes of some serious, classical concertos I've been working on over the past year and a half. It has absolutely nothing to do with pop music at all."

But whether he's working on neo-classical or popular rock, Michael Omartian will be keeping busy, putting into practice Stormie's words from their song, "One Song Is Not Enough."

One song is not enough,
You need more when the going gets rough.
You sing the blues when times are tough,
But one song is not enough.

You need songs of love
And songs of praise.
You need brand-new songs every day.
So forsake your style
Go the extra mile,
Let Jesus be your song of life
In every way.

Stryper (*left to right*): Tim Gaines (bass), Michael Sweet (guitar and lead voice), Robert Sweet (drums), and Oz Fox (guitar).

Chapter Six

STRYPER

Heavy metal is an ear-numbing, bone-crunching, guitar-dominated style of rock and roll popularized by bands like Led Zeppelin, Black Sabbath, AC/DC, Van Halen, and Scorpions.

Many heavy metal bands fill their songs with the praises of Satan, sex, and violence. And some bands show in both their on-stage and off-stage antics that they aren't trying to win any awards for virtue: The band W. A. S. P. showers its concert audiences with pieces of raw meat; while David Lee Roth, who started out singing for Van Halen, has publicized the fact that he has insurance to protect him from paternity suits.

It's not surprising, then, that critics of rock have few nice things to say about heavy metal. Its lyrics are often nasty, its music videos often violent, and its decibel levels potentially hazardous.

So we should turn our backs on this devilish music and consign the musicians to the pits of hell. Right?

Not according to four on-fire Christians from Southern California who make up Stryper. These four Christian rockers are known as heavy metal missionaries.

They play heavy metal, sure, but instead of singing about the devil they sing about Jesus their Lord.

Instead of inciting lust, they preach love.

Instead of bragging about how bad they are, they humbly talk about how good God is.

And instead of throwing raw meat from the stage they throw New Testaments and tracts. In fact, they say they have thrown more than thirty thousand Testaments into their crowds in the past year alone.

They don't play in churches or make records for a Christian label. In the world but not of it, they share the stage with bands with names like Sin and Anthrax and record for the

A Gradual Overnight Success

Stryper made its debut performance in February 1984. That fall the band was playing at the Troubador, a Los Angeles club with room for five hundred people. Now Stryper headlines dates at concert halls that seat ten to fifteen thousand people.

It sounds like the standard overnight success story. But behind the story is a more complicated tale that includes years of work and prayer.

Before there was Stryper there was Roxx, a band started in 1977 by guitarist and singer Michael Sweet and his brother Robert, who plays drums. Back then Michael was only fourteen years old, Robert was seventeen, and a big concert was a backyard party or high school dance. The Sweet brothers, who grew up in a family of professional musicians, had been playing instruments since before they could walk.

The brothers, along with the rest of the family, had accepted Jesus in 1975 because of a Jimmy Swaggart telecast. But for Michael and Robert, the rewards of godliness didn't seem as exciting as the fame and wealth they could win with their music. So they put Jesus on the back burner and concentrated on rock and roll.

Los Angeles-based Enigma label, the same label that launched Ratt and Motley Crue, two million-selling heavy metal bands.

If you want to know what they're about, listen to the words from their song, "From Wrong to Right."

> I've changed my ways from wrong to right.
> The devil never pays, he robs like a thief in the night.
> So many bands give the devil all the glory.
> It's so hard to understand, we want to change the story.
>
> We want to rock one way, on and on.
> You'll see the light some day.
> All say Jesus is the way.

Or just ask the band's drummer, Robert Sweet:

> We are rock and roll evangelists. The number one thing is to tell people about Jesus—especially the young kids—in a way they can relate to.
>
> When you're in court, both sides have an attorney, but in rock and roll or the entire secular music business today, no one tells God's side of the story. No one stands up for what's right. Everyone is standing up for your standard sex, drugs, drinking, adultery, Satanic worship, la, la, la.

The standard rock fare is something the members of Stryper understand well—it's what they were playing before they got straight with God.

Soon Oz Fox, a talented guitarist who had gone to high school with the Sweets, joined the band. Then, in 1981, the band's name was changed to Roxx Regime. "There were already a couple of bands named Roxx," says Michael. Together the band members worked even harder to make it to the top of the L. A. music heap.

But their long-desired success never came. Roxx Regime played gig after gig but never got the crowds, the record contract, or the fame they were striving for. Then one night during rehearsal they were confronted with the key to success—both for the band and their personal lives. As Robert tells it,

> We were rehearsing, and Ken Metcalf, a friend we had known, came in and said, "If you change your group around and glorify Jesus, you'll go straight to the top."
>
> We rededicated our lives to the Lord, and we said we don't care if none of the record companies wants to sign us or if none of the clubs wants to mess with a Christian band; this is what we're going to do.

The confrontation and the resulting change of hearts later helped to inspire the song, "You Know What to Do."

Are you feeling lonely?
Are you feeling blue?
Does your life seem empty?
You know what to do.

We've found a life that keeps us happy.
Yes we have, and we'll live eternally.
We'll always have a light to see, and so can you.

As soon as they focused on God and forgot about their own ambitions good things started to happen.

The band's lineup was completed with bassist Tim Gaines, the son of a Presbyterian minister and a Christian who had come to know God after a bout with suicidal despair.

The band's name was changed to Stryper.

The lyrics in all their songs, which had previously been standard appeals to partying, having a good time, and rocking and rolling, were rewritten to reflect the four members' commitment to Christ and spreading His message.

Then the new band with the new name, made up of musicians with new hearts, did something they had done many times before: They took a demo tape to Enigma Records. But this time Enigma agreed to put out their album—a six-song release with the title *The Yellow and*

Black Attack, named for the band's colors—yellow and black—which cover everything from their unique spandex outfits, to their instruments and stage settings.

Yellow and black attack indeed! Just as their friend had told them—they were on their way to the top.

Loud and Clear

Listening to a Stryper record or watching a Stryper concert, one immediately becomes aware of several things.

First, these guys cook. We're not talking just simmer or medium warm here, but boiling, smoldering, power-driven rock.

But there's more than raw, untrained power. There's finesse. The members of Stryper are arguably better musicians than members of Ratt, Motley Crue, Iron Maiden, and other bands who confuse volume with musical power, screaming with singing, bombast with truth.

Vocalist Michael Sweet wraps his vocal cords around a handful of octaves and styles, singing everything from the rock anthem, "Co'mon Rock," to the band's unique version of "The Battle Hymn of the Republic." On ballads like "Together as One," his vocals are smooth and flawless. Sweet takes command of the stage, giving an energetic performance that is masculine but not erotic.

And he plays a mean lead guitar, too.

Michael Sweet: Stryper's lead voice, main songwriter, and visual centerpiece.

Brother Robert says his goal has been to play drums like Eddie Van Halen plays guitar, and he seems to have hit the mark. Sitting in a drum chair with "Jesus Christ Rocks" printed on the back, Robert makes his drum set talk, punctuating the band's songs with a pounding bass drum, crashing cymbals, and fluid solos.

Oz Fox leads the guitar assault, tossing his head and curly long black hair as he stabs the air with stratospheric lead guitar breaks. And bassist Tim Gaines gives the music a bottom, adding background vocals to the mix.

The four members of Stryper are dedicated to their music, and it's the music that caught the attention of Enigma Records.

It's the music that is getting the attention of heavy metal fans—both religious and anti-religious—throughout the land.

It's the music that earned *Soldiers Under Command* a stay of twenty-three consecutive weeks on *Billboard* magazine's "Top Pop Albums" listing of the nation's two hundred best-selling records.

And it's the music that brought the band attention from magazines like *Rolling Stone, Circus, Spin, Time,* and *Newsweek.*

But Stryper's music is more than music to the four members of the band. It is their ministry. Their lyrics talk about Jesus, and how He came to save us from sin. On songs like "Loud 'n' Clear," the message comes through, well, loud and clear:

> *The hair is long and the screams are loud 'n' clear.*
> *The clothes are tight, earrings dangling from their ears.*
> *No matter how we look, we'll always praise His name.*
> *And, if you believe, you've got to do the same.*

The band's second album, *Soldiers Under Command,* presents an even bolder lyrical attack, as in the title song:

> *We are the soldiers under God's command*
> *We hold His two-edged sword within our hands*
> *We're not ashamed to stand up for what's right*
> *We win without sin, it's not by our might*
> *And we're fighting all the sin*
> *And the good book . . . it says we'll win*

or in the chorus to the song, "Makes Me Wanna Sing":

> *Jesus, King of Kings*
> *Jesus, makes me wanna sing*

or in the chorus to "Surrender":

> *Oh, Jesus Christ is the lover of your soul*
> *And He wants to give you all you need*
> *So freely surrender*
> *Open up unto His Majesty*

Although Stryper has been known as a heavy metal band, such a description is limiting and unfair. *Soldiers Under Command* contains not one but two touching ballads: "First Love" and "Together as One."

Singer Michael Sweet is the band's principal songwriter, contributing eleven of the sixteen songs on the band's two records, and co-writing four of the remaining five.

Sweet's musical influences—artists like Lionel Ritchie and Boz Scaggs—aren't the kind you would expect of someone interested only in heavy metal. He also likes the group Survivor. "Their songs are put together so well," he says. But, ultimately, Sweet has a completely different inspiration:

"When I sit down to write a song, I always pray. I don't want to sing; I don't want to write. I want God to sing and write through me, and to use me as an instrument."

And don't expect Stryper's songs to become less bold in the future:

> We really feel it's important to use the word *Jesus* in our songs, because that's what Christianity is all about—Jesus, who died to save us.
>
> A lot of ministries feel they should hold back and not be so bold. That's fine if that's what they are called to do. I don't think every Christian needs to shout Jesus from the rooftops. But we, as Stryper, have been called to do that and that's why we do it. We want to do it, and let people know about Him.
>
> And that's the reason why our career grows. The bolder we are, the more the Lord can use us and the bigger it gets.
>
> We try not to hit people over the head with Jesus. We do it in a way people can enjoy. There's good songs, a good beat, and we sing it in a way people can relate to. We say, "Hey, think about it."

Meet the Press

It's not every day that four young born-again Christians decide to marry the message of the gospel to heavy metal rock, and the world press has been quick to report on Stryper's unique musical ministry.

And it's not every day, either, that four Christian rockers are featured on shows like "America" and NBC's "American Almanac," and in every sort of magazine from *Hustler* to *Christianity Today*. But the band members are just as bold on national TV as they are in their songs.

Robert Sweet: Plays drums like Eddie Van Halen plays guitar.

Reporters, many of whom expect the band to be a group of money-hungry gimmick mongers, are confronted with a group of deeply committed Christians.

Here are some of the reports:

—*Circus* magazine said: "If you think that all L. A.-based metal bands can only rant about sex, drugs and more sex, you're in for a surprise."

—*Spin* called Stryper's music, "High-energy, knee-bending, hand-shaking, head-twisting heavy-metal rock with the power and glory of God."

—The *Los Angeles Times* reported: "The band gets sullen fans of Twisted Sister cheering and poking stubby 'one way' fingers heavenward—a refutation of the double-fingered 'devil horns' salute of many metal groups."

—*Contemporary Christian Magazine* said: "When the music stops for a vocal fill, you half-expect Ronnie James Dio to sing something like, 'Have an evil day.' What comes out instead is, 'Jesus is the way!' "

—*Billboard* called Stryper: "The first spandex-swathed, blatantly Christian heavy metal band" which "roars out songs with clean-cut lyrics about rockin' and salvation."

—*Rolling Stone* called them "heavy-metal Bible belters," and *Rock* magazine out of Los Angeles called them "head-bangers for God."

Befitting Stryper's growing worldwide popularity, the foreign press threw in its few sixpence worth.

England's *Kerrang!* wrote: "Stryper represents something of a Black Metal backlash. 'Jesus is the way,' they say, and who can knock their approach when the music is as strong as this?"

Not all the coverage Stryper has received has been friendly. *Time* magazine, for example, featured a photo of the colorfully clad band with this caption: "Dressed to save: Stryper gets set to sing the Word," and the accompanying article said they looked like their name could be the Killer Bees, with their yellow-and-black outfits adorned "with enough dangling chains to tie up half the elephants in Africa."

Like other events in the band's increasingly frantic and visible career, such publicity is taken in stride.

"Everybody has different kinds of publicity," says Michael Sweet, "and whatever kind of group you are you're going to get good publicity and bad publicity. We get our share of bad publicity, where people think we're a gimmick and they're trying to make fun of us, but that doesn't stop us. We just go on, because we know our calling is to spread the gospel of Christ. We can't let it get us down. We don't dwell on it."

Meet the Lions

If Stryper thought the reception they got at the hands of the press was bad, they should have waited until people in the church got wind of them.

Stryper's music took the argument that no form of music is inherently evil to what some would call its logical (or some might say illogical) extremes, and the band's unusual outfits only served to further inflame the church's long-running debate about rock and roll.

Reaction was instantaneous in California where Stryper's reputation first spread. Concerned Christians picketed the group's appearances as well as Christian bookstores that sold their records.

Like lions attacking first-century believers, many Christians went after these decidedly twentieth-century evangelists. One well-meaning brother even called Stryper's office to complain about the band's unprecedented Bible-distributing practice. He got drummer Robert Sweet on the line.

> Someone called me up and said our intentions were good, but he really thought that our throwing Bibles out into the audience was disrespectful.
>
> I said, "Okay, which choice is better for you: Do you want to see Bibles sit in a box and collect cobwebs, or do you want to see them thrown out to people who need to read them?"
>
> Guess what? He hung up.

Some of the fiercest criticism, however, came in the form of letters to the editor after articles on Stryper appeared in *Christianity Today* and *Contemporary Christian Magazine*.

A *CT* reader rhetorically asked: "Is not the mixing of Christian and heavy metal a contradiction in contrasting ideologies? If we were to evangelize prostitutes, would we be expected to dress like them also?"

Another reader wrote, "Our missionaries bringing the gospel to the world do not dress as witch doctors to convert the natives."

One writer requested that his subscription to *CT* be canceled, adding: "An article about a Christian heavy metal band is the same as writing about a 'Christian' physician who performs abortions and says he makes an impact on the murderers of America who also perform abortions."

One *CCM* reader lovingly wrote: "After reading your article about Stryper . . . I felt sick inside that the Lord's church could ever digress to the point that this type of thing would even exist. I, for one, would like to say that the members of Stryper look like a bunch of low-life scum buckets."

Daryn Hinton was another violent critic of Christian rock. She lived in the same area as Stryper members and attended a church where sermons against rock were a frequent affair. One night she attended a Stryper concert to gather evidence on the band's evil deeds. But she left with evidence of a different kind.

Robert Sweet remembers the night well.

We were opening up a concert for Bon Jovi in the spring of 1984, and a lady came to accuse us of doing what we were doing as a gimmick.

She came to point a finger at us and was surprised to see God's Word going out like it was. She invested a large sum of money in the band right off the bat, and the next day she was stuffing envelopes for Stryper. She became a believer when she saw that young people were being reached for Jesus.

Another supporter is Raul Ries, pastor of the 6,500-member Calvary Chapel of West Covina, California, where some members of the band fellowship.

"These guys are pulling people out of hell," he told *Christianity Today.* "They've been coming to church here for a few years, and we've seen a lot of their fruits. They bring a lot of people here to fellowship. I've seen what they're doing in the nightclubs, and I believe these guys really have a commitment to Jesus Christ."

According to Robert Sweet, questions about what Stryper is doing are answered in concert: "People are against us because they've never seen this happening before. I mean, if Christians are looking around for places where sin is taking place, how much worse can it get than in the music business?"

Even Robert's "favorite envangelist," Jimmy Swaggart, is opposed to the idea of Christian rock.

"I know that Jimmy Swaggart is down on rock, and I don't blame him because there's very little good rock and roll left. But I think he will see that God can use whatever He wants to use."

Just taking a look at Stryper's mailbox, gives one the distinct impression that God can use the band's music. Michael reports the band receives between one hundred fifty and two hundred letters a day, and, according to Robert, many say things like, "We used to be into Black Sabbath, Motley Crue, and Ronnie James Dio, but now we have accepted Christ."

Michael agrees: "A lot of kids who aren't Christians say they listen to us or saw us in concert and they're changing their lives. We get a lot of suicide letters from kids who decided not to commit suicide. That's what life is all about—seeing lives changed. That's why Stryper is rocking."

Stryper continues to rock, and a growing audience of loyal supporters is attending the band's concerts and buying their recordings. The pace of their lives is becoming more hectic as more and more newspapers, magazines, and radio and television stations clamor for interviews.

But the band members aren't losing sight of the goal.

"The group is gettng more popular and we are getting busier," says Michael, "but we fellowship, go to church, read our Bibles, and seek the Lord before we get too busy, because this is His ministry."

Or, as Michael sings, He is "The Rock That Makes Me Roll."

They say that rock 'n' roll is strong
But, God's the rock that makes us roll
Don't need no drugs to help us push on
We've got His power in our souls

Chapter Seven

STEVE TAYLOR

Through the ages, God's people have turned to music for comfort.

Whether it was David's harp calming the nerves and passions of King Saul, American slaves finding strength in their spirituals, or churchgoers combining their voices on hymns every week—music has been able to calm even the most troubled heart.

What then are we to make of the music of Steve Taylor—music that is riddled with satire, quirky, tinged with more than a hint of new wave rock, and anything but comforting?

Watch out when Taylor sets his sights on some of our most revered Christian leaders. He calls them "brylcreem prophets" or "charlatans in leisure suits," and pokes holes in their teachings.

And Taylor doesn't write about familiar places found in Christian vacation guides. He takes us to Madame Tussaud's famed wax museum in London (which serves as an illustration of hell and judgment) and to the Reptile Gardens Curio Shop, a place located nowhere but in the songwriter's own fertile imagination.

He sings about spiritual battles, some of which even angels have not yet dared to view (like the duel with the devil in the backseat of a Chevy).

And his characters aren't all noble and virtuous. No, they try to get by with everything: marital infidelity, hypocrisy, abortion, suicide, and insanity. But they rarely succeed.

Even the religious folk that populate Taylor's songs have their faults. In fact, Taylor's three recordings present a virtual catalog of the ills and idiosyncrasies of the modern American church—everything from country-club Christianity, through church-supported racism, to spiritual pride.

Taylor upsets our most cherished traditions and focuses in on our most frequently ignored sins. No stones are left unturned; no sacred cows are left un-fricasseed. Everything

is called into question. And that's the point—or at least one of the points—in the music of this intense and complicated singer. As Taylor puts it,

> I want to communicate. I want people to question things. I want the non-Christians to open their minds to the idea that maybe a lot of them have been lied to about what Christianity is all about. Maybe the reason they've rejected Christianity is not because they're rejecting Jesus but because they're rejecting a hypocritical church.
>
> And for the Christians, I want them to think about what it means to be a Christian in today's society, how that affects everyday life, and what demands that makes on us as believers.
>
> I want to communicate the responsibility we have to live out our faith, so communication is the key. If that doesn't happen, I think I'm wasting my time.

But What's a Nice Preacher's Kid Like You Doing Singing Songs Like That?

Taylor doesn't sing about the church's ills out of hatred or anger, but out of love.

> I became a Christian at a very young age, about four or five, and I never went through a big period of rebellion or anything. I love the church and want it to be conformed to the image of Christ, so I don't do things with a chip on my shoulder.
>
> Actually, my church experience was great. My dad has been a preacher all my life. I know that some preachers' kids hear one thing on Sunday morning and see another thing the rest of the week at home, but my parents were very consistent with what they said and what they did. They were good examples for me.

Where, then, did Taylor get the raw material for a song like, "I Manipulate," which has this damning first verse:

> *Does your soul crave center stage?*
> *have you heard about the latest rage?*
> *read your Bible by lightning flash*
> *get ordained at the thunder crash*
> *build a kingdom with a cattle prod*
> *tell the masses it's a message from God*
> *where the innocent congregate*
> *I manipulate*

Steve played the janitor who started the "Meltdown (At Madame Tussaud's)" in his video for that song.

and a frighteningly familiar pair of lines in a later verse:

if you question what I'm teaching you
you rebel against the Father too

And where does Taylor get the ideas for a song like "This Disco (Used to Be a Cute Cathedral)"?

Sunday needs a pick-me-up?
here's your chance
do you get tired of the same old square dance?
allemande right now
all join hands
do-si-do to the promised boogieland
got no need for altar calls
sold the altar for the mirror balls
do you shuffle? do you twist?
cause with a hot hits playlist, now we say

This disco used to be a cute cathedral
where the chosen cha-cha every day of the year
this disco used to be a cute cathedral
where we only play the stuff you're wanting to hear

Steve says he gets his ideas anywhere he can, then combines them in unlikely and amazing ways.

> The main thrust of that song was country-club Christianity, and where a church preaches what people want to hear in order to draw a certain crowd. But it was inspired by an actual disco I investigated in New York City.
> It really used to be a church, but now it's a disco with two thousand people bouncing up and down on the sanctuary floor, video screens lowered down over the organ's pipes, and records being played from what used to be the pulpit.
> So I just imagined that this was a Sunday night and the deacons had just devised a new way of getting new members into the church. It's like the idea of country-club Christianity and trying to gear our services to the beautiful people when Jesus made it very clear He didn't come for the people who were well but for those who needed a doctor.

Likewise it wasn't Taylor's experience with his church that led to the writing of the bitingly satirical title song from his 1982 debut recording, "I Want to Be a Clone."

I'd gone through so much other stuff
That walking down the aisle was tough

But now I know it's not enough
I want to be a clone
I asked the Lord into my heart
They said that was the way to start
But now I've got to play the part
I want to be a clone

They told me that I'd fall away
Unless I followed what they say
Who needs the Bible anyway
I want to be a clone
Their language it was new to me
But Christianese got through to me
Now I can speak it fluently
I want to be a clone

Be a clone and kiss conviction goodnight
Cloneliness is next to Godliness right
I'm grateful that they show the way
'Cause I could never know the way
To serve Him on my own
I want to be a clone

Although these songs are not about personal problems, they are drawn from experience.

> A lot of these songs are not about my problems. If I had all the problems in all of the songs I've written I'd probably be in serious psychological trouble.
> But at the time I wrote the song I knew a lot of people who had become Christians during the Jesus Movement and they felt like they really weren't fitting into any churches because they weren't being accepted for who they were.
> My church experience was fine, but the song was written for those people who had problems fitting into a church because they had come from a counterculture background.
> A lot of my songs come from questioning things. Questions aren't an insult to God. If He's the Creator and the source of all knowledge then He is going to be encouraging our questions.
> I think a lot of the church's problems come about because of a lack of critical thinking. People accept religious traditions without checking to see if they're biblical. They accept whatever their religious leader says because he is the Religious Leader. They forget that we're all human and capable of mistakes. We're all susceptible to being seduced by power and leading other people astray—along with ourselves.

Singin' and Grinnin'

For Steve Taylor, the road to a career singing Christian rock was a long and winding one.

His first personal experience with music was in fourth grade when he took up the trombone, an instrument that—even though he played it for another eight years—he failed to master.

But then, inspiration hit!

"In high school I realized that the one way you could attract girls if you weren't on the football team was to play in a rock band." So Taylor picked up the bass, laying down bass lines in garage bands until his graduation from high school in 1976.

Then it was off to Biola University, a Christian liberal arts college in California where Taylor studied the Bible and rediscovered his faith.

> At Biola I had a crisis of faith, wondering if all this stuff about Christianity was true or not. A Christian college can be very beneficial, but I felt so isolated from the world that I started wondering if I had been fed a line all of my life. It was at this time I did a lot of checking out of the historical claims of Christianity—reading people like Josh McDowell and Francis Schaeffer while trying to do my own research as well. At that time I decided Christianity was credible.

It's a good thing, because Taylor's next stop was the University of Colorado in Boulder, a type of Babylon of the Rockies.

"Going to Boulder from Biola was the biggest possible jump I could have made between two extremes," he says. "U. C. had picked up where Berkeley left off in the sixties. Every weekend the students would say, what are we going to protest this weekend?"

While Taylor studied for his B. A. degree in music and theater, another opportunity came his way—an opportunity that would change his life and outlook.

> When I got back to Colorado, the youth pastor of my father's church announced that he was going to leave to finish his education. The Board of Deacons asked me to fill in for him for a few months. I wound up filling in for five years. I was only nineteen when I started that position—barely much older than a lot of the kids in the group.
>
> I really enjoyed youth work, and it was during this time of going to college and serving as the church's youth pastor that I realized two things.

> First, I saw that music was the language of my culture. That was it. If you wanted to get through to kids you did it with music. You don't try to hype sports figures anymore, and they don't listen to politicians. They listen to music and musicians.
>
> Second, I felt that music at that time was not communicating much of anything to them, and that included most of the so-called contemporary Christian music. So when I started to write I tried to take some of the things I had been teaching my kids in youth group and put them into a musical format that I liked.

But before Taylor could sing his songs, he had to sing a few by somebody else.

> It's a little embarrassing to talk about now, but in the summer of 1979 I attended John Davidson's Singer Summer Camp—yeah, John Davidson, the "Tonight Show" and nightclub singer.
>
> I heard about this camp on the "Tonight Show" and applied, even though I wasn't particularly interested in being a nightclub singer. I left the camp realizing I could write my own songs, and that I could do something that might catch people's ears. I wanted to be a communicator and I knew I had talents in that area. I thought that maybe God could take this desire to be on stage and use it for His glory.

Taylor would be on many stages between 1981 and 1983, but it would still be a while before he was there with his band and singing his songs.

In the summer of 1981 Taylor toured with Cam Floria's Continental Singers. In the fall of 1982 he left on a nine-month tour serving as director of the Jeremiah People, a Christian group that combined music and skits and had a profound effect on the satirical music Taylor would later write.

> I had seen the Jeremiah People since I was in junior high school at Youth for Christ rallies. They were always funny, they used music and good, pointed satire.
>
> They would go into a church and, because they were funny, they could get away with saying things the pastor could never get away with saying. For example, one of their skits was about the numbers game in the church—how some churches measure their success and effectiveness by how many people are in the pews.

Another skit featured a little girl sharing with the audience some of the comments her mother had made about a certain man who had attended their church that Sunday. Apparently the man was not as well dressed as most of the other people. He was on welfare. And the girl's mother told the man he would probably be happier at the church down the road.

I wasn't crazy about their music, but I loved their satire. They had a way of getting through to people, and they had an effect on my writing.

Youth Pastor Meets the Clash

But not all of the influences on Taylor's unique writing style came from within the walls of the church.

After the John Davidson camp I realized how bored I was with pop music in general. Then new wave and punk music started trickling over from England, and it really caught my ear.

The band that had the biggest influence on me was the Clash. I never doubted for a minute that they believed what they were singing about. I didn't agree with a lot of it, but they yelled out the words with such conviction and fire. Also, in their interviews you could tell that they were really trying to live out what they were singing about.

I thought, *Well, if I'm a Christian and I know about ultimate truth, I want to write songs with the same kind of conviction and power behind them.* And I also knew that new wave music was, essentially, four guys getting together who couldn't play musical instruments, and that appealed to me because I couldn't play anything either.

Everybody Must Get Cloned

Late in 1979 Taylor started writing his songs, and before the year was out he gathered together some musician friends from the Denver area, went to a budget studio, and started recording demo tapes of his new music. The next step was to send out tapes to record companies and wait for the rejection slips.

"One company thought it was too crazy, another company thought the music was a passing fad, another said they preferred to stay away from controversial subjects like abortion," recalls Steve.

The break came in 1982, right before he hit the road with Jeremiah People. Cam Floria, organizer of an annual Christian music festival in Estes Park, Colorado, invited

The "Meltdown" video took Taylor's vision of divine judgment to MTV and other video shows.

Taylor to play two songs. So Steve and his band took the stage to play "I Want to Be a Clone" and "Whatcha Gonna Do When Your Number's Up?" The songs were well received and Sparrow Records signed Taylor on the spot. His six-song debut was hurriedly recorded before Jeremiah People began their tour.

Much to almost everyone's surprise, *I Want to Be a Clone* took off, selling very well for a debut by a youth pastor artist who sang about Christian clones and—in the song "Steeplechase"—church-swappers:

A change of habit
Used to go bar-hopping
You started church-shopping did ya
It's been a problem
Finding one to fit ya
You didn't feel good did ya

You like the big ones
Worship incognito
Your problems ain't getting solved
You try a small one
Oops you must retreat-o
You'd rather not get involved

It's a steeplechase
Blame your failures
On churches where you've gone
Steeplechase
Ice-cold Christian fakes
Turn to frosted flakes

The album also included "Whatever Happened to Sin?" and "Written Guarantee," two songs that Taylor still plays in concert.

"The album caught on real quickly," he says. "It was cheap, a mini-LP, so it cost less than a regular album. And it seemed to hit a nerve. The content seemed to separate it from a lot of what was going on in Christian music."

But Taylor isn't sure he was surprised the album did well:

"It's one of those things where, on the one hand you're surprised; but, on the other hand, the only way you're able to keep doing what you're doing the whole time is that you keep telling yourself it's going to happen."

The success wasn't merely a one-time thing. Taylor's wry humor, his courage to look sin in its ugly face, and his jumpy music won fans for following albums as well.

Meltdown, released in 1984, included ten songs instead of six. The album sounds like more care was taken in the recording studio, and it shows that Taylor's writing and singing skills had matured.

"Meltdown (At Madame Tussaud's)," the album's opening cut, painted a vivid picture of what judgment day would be like for the rich and famous by showing what happens to the characters' wax figures when someone accidentally sets the thermostat too high (" 'Howard Hughes—Billionaire' says the written guide/pity that his assets have all been liquified").

The "Meltdown" video, which highlighted Taylor's acting abilities, was supremely done and was shown on MTV, a rarity for Christian music videos.

The album's second song, "We Don't Need No Colour Code," was a rollicking rock number that found Taylor focusing in on his Christian targets while honing his writing skills to present just the right mixture of humor and truth.

> *Down Carolina way lived a man name ol' Big B.J.*
> *B.J. went and got a school founded on caucasian rule*
> *Bumper sticker on his Ford says "Honkies If You Love the*
> *   Lord"*

The song's final verse took a look at South Africa's doctrine of apartheid and brought it all back home to the Bible:

> *Marching to Pretoria*
> *colour codes in churches huh?*
> *following a fascist creed*
> *whose translation do you read?*
> *true believers won't be snowed*
> *we don't need no colour code*

Meltdown also hounded the media in "Meat the Press" ("a Christian can't get equal time / unless he's a looney committing a crime"); took a look at Soviet repression of Poland in "Over My Dead Body" (a song that was later broadcast behind the Iron Curtain by Voice of America);

told the story of "Jenny," a young girl who takes her own life after getting lost in the big city; and asked where young people could go for positive role models in "Hero" ("Growing older you'll find that illusions are bought / and the idol you thought you'd be was just another zero").

Pretty heavy stuff for a Christian album, right? But Taylor wasn't through. He also looked at casual sin in "Sin for a Season."

> *There's a sweaty hand handling his cocktail napkin*
> *"come on up and see me" is scribbled with a gold pen*
> *"but you'd better ring twice"*
> *seven months after his little indiscretion*
> *he sits with his wife in a therapy session*
> *for a little advice*
> *"If the healing happens as the time goes by*
> *tell me why I still can't look her in the eye"*
> *"God I'm only human, got no other reason . . ."*
> *sin for a season*

"Guilty by Association" tackled the issue of Christian cliquishness (". . . let your fingers take a walk / through the business guide for the 'born again' flock"), examined television evangelists who continually wring money out of their weary supporters ("It's a Telethon Tuesday for 'The Gospel Club' / 'send your money in now or they're gonna pull the plug!' "), and critiqued Christian critics of rock music:

> *Turn the radio on to a down-home drawl*
> *hear a brylcreem prophet with a message for y'all*
> *"I have found a new utensil in the devil's toolbox*
> *and the heads are gonna roll if Jesus rocks*
> *it's of a worldly design! God's music should be divine!*
> *try buying records like mine—avoid temptation"*
> *guilty by association*
>
> *So you say it's of the devil and we've got no choice*
> *because you heard a revelation from the "still small voice"*
> *if the Bible doesn't back it then it seems quite clear*
> *perhaps it was the devil who whispered in your ear*

On the Fritz, released in 1985, carried Taylor's work a bit further, but musically the album was a departure. Instead of the Denver musicians who had appeared on his previous recordings, Taylor hired some of New York's top session players. The album was produced by Ian McDonald, a founding member of both Foreigner and King Crimson.

Following the opening cut, "This Disco," the album's title cut looked at Christian musicians who fall victim to spiritual pride ("if you don't die to yourself / pride kills"); while "You've Been Bought" takes an equally

hard look at the sexually violent image of secular musicians ("did you slap around the ladies for the camera? / do you slap 'em when the camera isn't there?").

"It's a Personal Thing" pokes fun at public figures who clothe themselves in religious garb only when convenient; "Lifeboat" is a hilariously sad look at a values clarification game Taylor played as a student in public schools, later made into a music video ("We've learned our lesson—teacher says perfection's what counts"); "I Manipulate" questions the teachings of the Bill Gothard school of absolute hierarchies and authority ("... a good wife learns to cower / underneath the umbrella of power"); while "You Don't Owe Me Nothing" criticizes those who capitalize on Christianity:

> There was a time in Christendom
> the road to God was hard to tread
> 'til charlatans in leisure suits
> saw dollars dancing in their heads

On the Fritz also included a touching song on the power of grace, "To Forgive," and a hauntingly beautiful song of dedication to God, "I Just Wanna Know," but again it was the album's more controversial, pointed songs that caused controversy.

Blessings From a Church Father

Even though Steve Taylor's music pokes a pointed finger at some of the church's foibles, he still has some support among the clergy. For an official and theologically accurate assessment of the singer's work we went to a respected pastor, Reverend Roland Taylor of Crossroads Baptist Church in Denver, a dedicated minister who just happens to be the singer's father.

> I think what Steve is doing is merely challenging some of the things that are being promoted as a basis of Christianity.
> I think everybody needs to realize that they're going to be subjected to some criticism, and some of these people are in Steve's songs. But I don't think, for example, that he is anti-Bill Gothard. We have attended Gothard's seminars and feel that much of what he has to say is very worthwhile. But I think a person can become too wrapped up in his own approach to theology, and I think there are places where Bill Gothard needs to be challenged.

And although Reverend Taylor is not an avid rocker, he doesn't see Scripture directing his son or others to avoid rock.

> Music is constantly changing. When Martin Luther wrote "A Mighty Fortress Is Our God,"

the tune he used and which is still used in our churches today was a bar tune of that day. And Isaac Watts was critical of the staid songs of his church.

Likewise, I look at Steve's music as a means of communicating a message to our generation today. The young people aren't going to listen to the words of a song their forefathers listened to. It's like going to a foreign country. You may not appreciate the sounds the people there make, but those are the sounds in which they communicate to each other.

In America we're separated by a great barrier of age, and we need to be able to communicate the message of the gospel to our young people who aren't going to hear it unless we do it in their language and their type of music.

Salt, Light, and Wit

Can a former PK (preacher's kid) and youth worker find happiness in the rough and tumble world of modern music? Apparently so, and Taylor is using the platform his music has given him to address more young people than could fit into any church basement on a Saturday night.

I want to encourage my generation to think. When I was in college it seemed like I was seeing a lot of kids who grew up in the church going off to college and coming back six months later wondering why they ever believed in Christianity in the first place. I don't want to see that happen—I believe the Christian faith has answers, so I encourage them to ask questions and to put their faith into action.

Since being a rock musician seems to often include being a role model as well, I hope I can be a good one. I take that responsibility very seriously, because when I was growing up, I needed examples too.

A Christian rocker/humorist/satirist as an example for American youth?
Would you prefer Twisted Sister?

Steve teamed up with Sheila Walsh for the "Taylor/Walsh Transcontinental Tour '85."

Petra 1986 (*left to right*): John Lawry (keyboard), Bob Hartman (guitar), Louie Weaver (drums), Mark Kelly (bass), and John Schlitt (lead voice).

Chapter Eight

PETRA

I t's early 1986, and Petra is journeying down under in Australia.

The members of the band—guitarist Bob Hartman, bassist Mark Kelly, keyboardist John Lawry, drummer Louie Weaver, and new lead vocalist John Schlitt—are en route to a concert where they will present their international, nondenominational, high-decibel offering of music and good news.

Of course, the realities of the road are nothing new to these guys. Hartman has gone hundreds of thousands of miles with his guitar and his songs since he founded Petra in Indiana in 1972. Since then, Petra has earned its reputation as one of the hardest-working, farthest-traveling bands in the land—bar none.

And the road is nothing new to Schlitt. Although this is his first time out with Petra, the veteran vocalist toured long and hard with Head East, the popular rock band he fronted during its heyday between 1975 and 1980.

The world of rock is full of stories and songs about the terrors of travel—the tight quarters, the white highway lines blurring into sorry sameness, the repeated packing and unpacking of luggage and sound equipment, the anxiety borne of this vagabond existence, and the seemingly interminable distances between brief stops.

But the members of Petra don't let it get them down. They don't savor the road but they endure it as a necessary evil, for these are minstrels with a mission, troubadors for the truth.

Many miles and many hours later, when Petra hits the stage, it all becomes worth it—both for members of the band and the audience.

As sound, light, and smoke pour from the stage, more than five thousand people jump, scream, applaud, wave, and sing along. And as band and audience repeat a well-known chorus, it's obvious that this isn't your typical rock fare:

Without Him we can do nothing.
Without Him we can do nothing.

If there is any question about the "Him" the band and their audience are singing about, the next song provides the answer:

Praise ye the Lord.
Praise ye the Lord.
Praise ye the Lord forever.
Praise ye the Lord.
Praise ye the Lord.
Praise ye the Lord forever.

Then, without pause, Petra launches into a rock version of Handel's "Hallelujah Chorus," full of sound and praises to God. It's not your typical rock concert, but then Petra—which is Greek for "rock"—is not your typical band.

"For me the name Petra has a dual meaning," says Bob Hartman, the band's founder, chief songwriter, and guitarist. It means rock music, but it also means that we stand upon the rock of our belief in Christ, like Peter in the Book of Matthew, where Christ said, 'Upon this rock I will build my church.' "

It was 1972 when Hartman and three of his Bible school friends first took to the stage as Petra. Since then, the band has undergone all manner of trials and tribulations: numerous personnel changes, frequent financial crises, continual criticism of the band's style of music, and even occasional discussions about giving up the whole thing altogether.

But Petra, like some indestructible boulder, has endured—selling more than a million records and playing for millions of receptive listeners.

Petra's story is one of faith, perseverance, love, and music.

God Gave Us Rock

The story begins with a boy and his guitar. Bob Hartman's love for music was obvious at an early age.

> I have been playing the guitar since I was thirteen years old. I played guitar throughout high school and college. When I was twenty, I met the Lord. But even long before that, I can remember being so thankful I could play the guitar. It gave me such joy and satisfaction that I wanted to thank somebody for being able to play. The only one I knew to thank was God.
>
> I didn't have a real strong belief in God then,

Bob Hartman

but I knew that talent and ability must come from someplace, and the only place I could think of was God.

So I thanked God for it.

When Hartman graduated from college in 1972, he desired a type of knowledge he hadn't heard about in his classes. He wanted to learn to understand the Bible and to tell others about it. As he puts it, "I feel I was called to the ministry."

He enrolled at Christian Training Academy, a sort of Christian junior college in Fort Wayne, Indiana. There he met three believers who shared his commitment to spreading the gospel and his enthusiasm for guitar-based rock.

Hartman joined forces with guitarist Greg Hough, bassist John DeGroff, and drummer Bill Glover—and Petra was born.

The band's music was, as Hartman admits now, "primitive." Their high-decibel approach to music evangelism consisted of piercing guitar riffs punctuated by crashing drums and cymbals and a throbbing bass line.

Even though rock was still considered the devil's music by many in the church, friends and teachers at the Christian Training Academy knew the four ministering minstrels were sincere in wanting to communicate the gospel through music, so they offered encouragement and support.

Soon, Petra was packing up its gear and traveling to schools, colleges, parks, and prisons throughout the area, bringing to all a loud encounter of the religious kind.

Says Hartman,

> Rock music began in a culturally rebellious way. It was, "You older people have your music, and now we have our music. You don't like ours, and that makes us like it all the more."
>
> Some people have pointed to that and said, "See, this is where rock began. How can God use it, because it all began in rebellion?"
>
> But rock has now become a standard of music—it *is* popular music. And we think it is a good way to communicate to the people who listen to it.

By 1973, Petra had become a regional sensation. People came from all around to attend the band's concerts at The Adam's Apple, a Fort Wayne Christian center. Soon the band began traveling greater distances, expanding their loyal audience.

Later that year came their first opportunity to become a truly national band: Representatives from Myrrh, Word

Louie Weaver

Records' new contemporary label, wanted Petra to record an album.

The band's debut album, *Petra*, was released in 1974. Although it was a good beginning for Christian hard rock, the album suffered from many problems: The band was inexperienced in a recording studio; and producer Billy Ray Hearn, who was heading up the Myrrh label after years as a church music director, failed to capture Petra's in-person pizzazz on vinyl.

After it was released, the album faced more problems. Word Records saw *Petra* as an experimental record in the brave new world of Christian rock, and was waiting to see what happened in the marketplace.

What happened first was that many Christian bookstores refused to carry the record. Although some bookstores did carry it, often under the counter, 1974 was still too early for this kind of music. Petra's head-banging rock wasn't what consumers and booksellers expected from a Christian quartet. And Hartman wasn't going to receive any Grammy awards for his vocals, or for the lyrics he wrote for nine of the album's ten songs. "Walkin' in the Light," for example, featured the profound refrain:

> *Walkin' in the light, every day and night*
> *Livin' in the Spirit, really out of sight.*

After a decade with Petra, singer Greg Volz left in 1985 to pursue a solo ministry.

But Petra played on, and in 1977, Myrrh released their second album, *Come and Join Us.*

The band had hoped this harder-edged release would bridge the gap to secular record buyers just as the band's concerts had reached many of the nonbelievers in the crowd. They even recorded their version of "God Gave Rock and Roll to You," a song by the secular band Argent (which also appears on Petra's *Beat the System* album) and recruited veteran vocalist Greg Volz to handle the singing.

Instead of paving Petra's way to greater acceptance, the record met with violent reaction. Although many Christian rockers welcomed the album, some older Christians hated it more than they had Petra's debut recording. The hoped-for secular sales never materialized.

After *Come and Join Us*, Myrrh decided the hard rock experiment had failed. Petra was without a label or recording contract.

Miles, Aisles, and Trials

The seventies were trying times for Petra and other Christians who played rock music. Although *Time* magazine and *Rolling Stone* had done stories about "the Jesus Movement" in 1971, the movement was still young and was carried forward more by youthful sentiment than by mature commitment.

In 1975, just one year after Petra's debut album caused a stir, Randy Matthews, Myrrh Records' first recording artist, was unplugged mid-set at the Jesus '75 festival because promoters felt his raucous rock sounded demonic.

Throughout this period, well-intentioned but poorly planned bands, record labels, and magazines dedicated to Christian rock went bankrupt and folded. But Hartman and company kept on "keeping on." Although success would have been nice, that wasn't their reason for playing. They were musical ministers, and they were convinced they were where God wanted them to be. As Hartman recalls,

> Those years were rough for us. This was before there was such a thing as a Christian concert circuit. There weren't any managers or booking agents, and although there were some good things about this, generally it was very hard on the artists.
>
> I heard horror stories about bands that drove eight to ten hours to get to a concert and then received only one dollar in offering. There were times we in Petra literally didn't have any food to eat. On three occasions we were written bad checks by Christian promoters who didn't tell us they didn't have the money to cover the checks. That would hurt our band and personal finances for months.

Band members couldn't make a living from Petra's concert and record earnings, and all had to juggle jobs and relationships to keep the band together. For a while, it seemed as if the tension might destroy the band from within.

"But we knew that God had called us to do what we were doing," says Hartman, "or else we wouldn't have done it. We *couldn't* have done it."

With his firm belief in the band's calling, Hartman kept Petra alive, and eventually began to see glimpses of success. But he couldn't maintain the band's original lineup. Original members Hough, Glover, and DeGroff left and were replaced by other able musicians. Hartman also persuaded Greg Volz to join the band full-time. Volz, who had contributed vocals to *Come and Join Us* and who had been offered a singing job with REO Speedwagon, instantly became a valuable part of the band's sound and show.

Volz, who left Petra in early 1986 to pursue a solo career, was a valuable part of the Petra sound. He also shared Hartman's sense of calling—that Petra was to minister the gospel to the masses:

We want to be an edification to the body of believers. We believe God has given us an ability to bring a release to people in their spirits and to free them to worship God in a new way, in a new realm, and to express themselves to the Lord.

But God has also given us a contemporary style of music in which we challenge the nonbeliever on his own ground, where he lives, with a common denominator he can understand, which is rock and roll.

God says all through the Scriptures that we are to excel in our gift, and not to be schlock. Psalms 33:3 says, "Sing to Him a new song; Play skillfully with a shout of joy."

If you can prove to someone that you're not some wacko out in left field—if a nonbeliever respects you as a musician—he'll listen to what you say. We're planting seeds, and sometimes we get to harvest those seeds too.

Even in the midst of personnel changes though, Petra didn't slow down, but continued its hectic touring schedule. In 1977 the band took more equipment than ever on the road to play more than a hundred gigs. Year by year, the band built up a loyal following across the country. By 1982 they were on the road three hundred days out of the year.

If there were any doubts left about why they were playing, the band's concerts held the answer. Night after night they belted out relevant and biblically based songs, and hundreds of the kids in the audience responded by giving their lives up to God.

Petra's albums held the answer too. *Never Say Die* included a number of hard-rocking, thought-provoking songs written by Hartman.

"Angel of Light" probed the devil:

> *Angel of light. I see you glow in the night.*
> *But you only bring darkness to my soul.*
> *Angel of light. You're tellin' me wrong is right.*
> *But I won't let your evil take control."*

"Chameleon" wasn't about reptiles; it took a hard look at believers who are both in the world and of it.

> *You want the best of both worlds,*
>   *but you're not getting either.*
> *You seem content to ride the fence*
>   *when you know which side is greener.*
> *Some run hot and some run cold*
>   *and some run from their maker.*
> *Some run the risk of losing all*
>   *with lukewarm friends and fakers.*

Mark Kelly

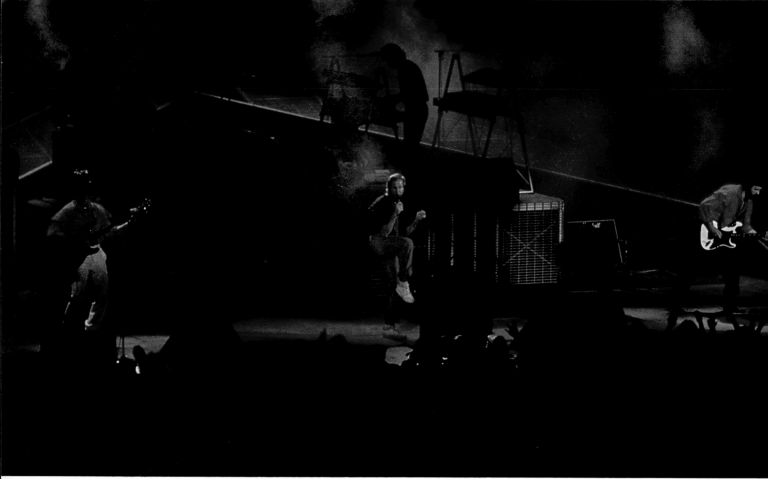

"Killing My Old Man" wasn't about family troubles and violent youthful rebellion, but about living a new life as a Christian while facing the temptations and memories of the old life:

I've really got to find a way of taking care of him for good.
I know he'd kill me if he could. So I'll nail him to the wood.

In concert these songs were delivered with powerful music from sincere hearts.

This Is War

Through eight albums and fourteen years of concerts, one theme seen in many of Petra's songs is the spiritual warfare that engulfs our world and all the souls who live here.

As the band's music has grown more sophisticated and professional, and as Hartman has become increasingly adept at writing contemporary expressions of timeless biblical truths, Petra has carried messages of sin and judgment, encouragement, and hope to hundreds of thousands of concertgoers and record buyers.

The imagery of war can be seen most readily on the album covers of the 1981 release, *Never Say Die*, which shows a guitar-shaped ship doing battle on stormy seas, and 1983's *Not of This World*, which shows Star Wars-type aircraft engaged in intergallactic battles.

The imagery has even shown up in the band's stage outfits, including camouflage-style fatigues and modernistic space suits. But Petra's theme of spiritual warfare appears most clearly in their lyrics. In the title song from their 1981 album, *Never Say Die*, Volz sang:

Never say die. You've come too far to turn back now.
Give it one more try and He'll help you through.
Never say die. We are weak, but He is strong and
Strength He will supply when you ask Him to.

In the title song from 1984's *Beat the System*, Hartman's meaty lyrics, which are carried by a contemporary-sounding synth-rock accompaniment, challenge the listener to persevere in the life of faith:

Caught in the undertow being swept downstream
Going against the flow seems like such a dream
Trying to hold your ground when you start to slide
Pressure to compromise comes from every side
Wise up Rise up
You can be more than a conqueror, you will never face defeat
You can dare to win by losing all, you can face the heat,
    dare to
Beat the System

*Opposite page:*Members of Petra meeting Yves Joseph, the Haitian child they sponsor through Compassion International.

Such songs, and the way the band performs them, confirm Hartman's view of Petra's calling: "We're not musicians who happen to be Christians, we're Christians who happen to be musicians. We are Christians and ministers, and we don't want to hide that fact. We want to be *blatantly* Christian."

And just as any experienced military strategist will try to fight the enemy on more than one front, Petra battles sin and faithlessness with more than music.

One important weapon in the Petra arsenal is Petra Ministries' quarterly newsletter, which is sent at a cost of more than thirty thousand dollars per issue to some two hundred thousand people who have requested it.

Although the newsletter is a good public relations tool for the band, and carries news about concert dates, T-shirts, albums, and other products, it also contains solid Bible studies and information on how listeners can get involved in the work of Compassion International.

Petra has been supporting Compassion International since 1984, and the album *Beat the System* contained an insert supporting the ministry for hungry children worldwide which read, "You can help a needy child 'beat the system.' "

Band members traveled to the troubled Caribbean nation of Haiti in 1985 to view Compassion's work there. The band's appeals in behalf of Compassion—whether through concert appearances, songs, or albums—have been responsible for thousands of people making commitments to sponsor Third World children through the international relief and development organization.

Bob Hartman wrote the song "Hollow Eyes" following the trip to Haiti:

In the crowded sheds the children lay their heads
To escape the Haitian heat
The hunger pains drive them to the street
Wondering today if they'll eat
Some find food in the refuse heap.

The song's haunting chorus asks: "Do you dare to gaze into their hollow eyes?"

Petra also shows compassion toward America's needy, offering complimentary passes to drug rehabilitation centers, handicapped and halfway houses, and orphanages. But the band's first calling is to minister through music—not through public relief efforts. And when they take to the road they take along enough equipment to support an entire musical army:

- Three 52-foot semi-trucks, with an additional 24-foot truck and two buses;
- Thirty-two sound cabinets carrying more than 15,000 watts of power;
- Four hundred lights with 400,000 watts of power, all run by a computerized control board;
- Ten tons of stage gear for suspending the lights and sound equipment in mid-air;
- A twenty-member crew of technicians and drivers.

After a concert is over, band members don't run from the audience. When conditions permit they hang around long enough to give autographs and counsel to many of the kids who line the stage to meet them. It's a simple gesture that helps show the ministers' love for their audience.

Petra has also recorded several music videos, a tactic that may expose additional ears and eyes to their ministering music.

A New Soldier Joins the Battle

In early 1986 Petra lost the services of Greg Volz, lead vocalist since the days of *Never Say Die.* Volz had decided to go solo, and it was again up to Hartman to find a new band member.

Some were surprised when John Schlitt, former vocalist for Head East, was chosen to replace Volz. Schlitt had not sung for four years and was a complete stranger to Christian music. But Hartman wasn't surprised:

> I had sat next to John once on a plane when he was flying to a Head East date. And Head East recorded their first album in the same studio with the same engineer that Petra used for its first album only months later.
>
> I had heard that John had become a Christian since leaving the band, and one day I spent a few hours trying to track him down. I found his brother's name on the back of Head East's "Flat As a Pancake" album and managed to locate him. He contacted John and John called me pretty quickly.

John's side of the story shows his desire to wait on God.

> I had totally given up on ever singing again, except for singing in church on Sunday. Between 1981 and 1985 I even made a point of not listening to the radio.
>
> I had worked as a floor sweeper, a mining engineer, and all sorts of jobs in the last five years. I told God, "Whatever You want me to do, I will do the best that I can." And God was honoring that. I was getting promotions and better jobs, but I still felt empty.
>
> About the time I finally laid down before God my desire to sing again, that was when my brother heard Bob was trying to get a hold of me.
>
> I know that I'm not up on Christian music, but that's okay. Everything that I'm doing now comes from my heart, not from a desire to be competitive with some other Christian artist.
>
> But the most important thing is the opportunity to make a difference in people's lives—to be a part of something that can change people. Rock and roll has become such a controlling factor in

so many lives. It's disgusting. But God designed music for His enjoyment and glory long ago. A thief came in and stole it, and we're stealing it back.

Saints and Sinners

A preacher once said that people can be divided into two groups—those who know God and those who don't. Petra's music is intended for both groups. The band's sound, developed and polished over years of practice, attracts all those who like rock; while the lyrics communicate to both the worldly and the other-worldly.

As Hartman explains,

> People get freed inside, and that's why we believe in gospel rock. Rock music is exciting music, and there are very many things to be excited about in being a Christian. When you put those things together and point them toward God, people get excited and there's a release.
>
> God made us body, soul, and spirit, and He intended the whole thing to be in relationship with Him—not just our spirits. He wants us to be excited and worship Him. That's why the Bible says "Clap your hands unto the Lord." That's why it says "Shout" or "Sing to the Lord." He wants us to use our physical bodies to worship Him.
>
> When that happens there's a strength that comes; there's a freedom that comes.

If things continue as they have been, Petra's records and concerts will be heard by increasingly larger audiences. The band may now be more able to achieve the goal which they had for their 1977 album *Come and Join Us*—to reach secular listeners. In 1985 Word Records, which—ironically—now distributes Petra's records for the independent Star Song Records label, signed an agreement with A&M Records, allowing A&M to distribute records by Petra and other Word artists to mainstream record stores.

Also in 1985, Petra began signing agreements with secular rock promoters to get the band into some of the nation's larger arenas and in front of audiences who need to know about God's love for them. As Hartman says:

> We believe that as we go forth in the name of the Lord, God will honor His Word; because it's God's Word that changes lives, not how good Petra is, how well we perform, or how we look on stage. God will do it.

Chapter Nine

RANDY STONEHILL

It's four o'clock in the afternoon on a dark and rainy Friday in Kansas City. Most people in the city are getting ready to go home, but Randy Stonehill is getting ready to go to work.

Although he doesn't have an office, a desk, or a timeclock, Randy has been working hard at the same job for fifteen years now. And on this afternoon in this city he does something he has done at least two thousand times before—he prepares to take the stage to sing his songs about life, love, and anything else that comes to his quick and inquisitive mind.

As he sips on hot tea ("It's good for the throat") and collects his thoughts and energy for the concert to come, Randy reflects on his unique vocation:

> Tours are a wonderful opportunity to actually look into the faces of the audience—the people you write and record for. It's no longer this sort of nebulous group of people out there somewhere. You're on stage and you try to give your heart—try to give something real. I try to save up all my energy, jump in, and give 105 percent. I love what I do, and I feel like if I'm not losing a lung or some vital organ for the audience I'm cheating them.
>
> I'm working on a song called "The Kid in the Third Row." I always imagine myself out there in a way, and I remember how I felt when I was in junior high and high school and going to a lot of concerts. I remember how closely I watched those people and how much joy they brought me and how much influence they had.
>
> That's a frightening responsibility to me, but it keeps me praying because I want to be a faithful servant. I want to be responsible with everything I do. Music moves people and cuts through their defenses, so I know that I have influence or leverage because I'm on the platform in a spotlight playing music.

This is what I'm called to do. I've worked long and hard at it, and I believe I'm good at what I do. I care about these people and what I'm doing because God cares.

The new song, "The Kid in the Third Row," isn't finished yet, so while he pulls on his shoes Randy does an a cappella version of a couple of verses from "I'll Remember You," the final song from the album *Celebrate This Heartbeat*:

> *I'll remember you*
> *No this isn't just another town I'm passing through*
> *Though I might not know you all by name*
> *The way I feel is still the same*
> *I believe the Lord has brought me here*
> *And I'm glad I came*
>
> *And before I go*
> *There's something very special that you all should know*
> *For the Lord of love is here with you*
> *And He'll fill your hearts if you ask Him to*
> *And I'm proud to be the one to share the happy news*
> *I'll remember you*
> *And He'll remember you*
> *I'll remember you*

The Other Side of the Road

That rainy day in Kansas City was an excellent time to test Randy Stonehill's dedication to his craft, his audience, and his God. And maybe a test isn't such a bad idea.

Lots of people question the sincerity of Randy and others who make music. These critics picture Christian musicians leading lives of simplicity and ease, with chauffeured limousines, luxury lodging, and all the self-centeredness and pride that such a life-style might encourage.

After all, it's easy to stand on stage and talk about one's dedication to "the ministry" of music, to gush about one's love for the hundreds of people out there who paid hard cash for the privilege of attending the concert. The question is, how does that dedication hold out when the rubber meets the road and the spotlight hits the stage?

As the rainy day turned into an equally rainy and bone chillingly cold evening, and as problem after problem seemed to develop, Randy and the tour entourage kept their faith and patience.

Oh, there was nothing wrong with the concert. Randy and the musicians gave at least 106 percent, and the audience roared its approval. Although Randy didn't lose any vital organs, he did give his knee a National Football League workout.

During the final verse of his hard-hitting song, "The

Gods of Men," Randy was banging his guitar and singing the lines: "And I used to dream of being a hero/ Yeah, I told myself I'd never fall down." Then, without warning, Randy fell backward and crashed to the stage. The band continued to play as Randy remained motionless, savoring the paradox between the song's words and his theatrical actions. Just as suddenly as he fell, he sprang back up to his feet and launched into the next lines of the song. But on the way up he twisted his knee. Probably no one in the audience noticed, but Randy still felt the pain hours after the show.

Aside from problems with his body, the appearance in Kansas City presented other problems as well:

—the concert was in an old opera house with backstage walls graced by the signatures of Loretta Lynn and Ferlin Husky where the promoters seemed more familiar with C & W than CCM;

—when the band arrived shortly after 4:00 P.M., the sound and light crews complained that they hadn't received the help they had been promised. As a result, concertgoers who came early to get good seats wound up waiting outside in—that's right—a rainy Kansas City evening as sound checks continued until well past 7:00 P.M.;

—Randy's dressing room, a small affair decorated with eye-jarring wallpaper that could induce hallucinations— even for people who never experimented with drugs— was a cool forty-five degrees, causing Randy to wear a jacket and scarf and cling to his thermos of hot tea;

—Randy's throat was sending him warning signals that it might become sore and unreliable, a situation not helped by the room's low temperature;

—there was a problem with concessions—the records and T-shirts that help to finance many a Christian concert tour. The promoter demanded either that he receive an unusually high percentage of these sales or that his employees handle the merchandise and cash;

—poor promotion, along with the weather, brought fewer than the expected number of people to the concert (although all present indicated their pleasure with the entire show);

—and, to top it all off, the band lost money on the appearance. The promoter said he was unable to come up with the money he had promised and would have to rely on his Christian brothers' willingness to "work it out," or something like that.

And there wasn't a limousine, luxury hotel, sumptuous feast, or groupie anywhere in sight!

So how did Randy feel about his calling that night?

Just fine, thank you.

"We lost money but we parted friends with those people, and that's really more important than the money," said Randy afterwards. "The money all comes from the Lord in the first place, so He will make up the difference with other shows where things work out better. As it turned out, the next night we were paid before we took the stage. I said, 'Thanks, God. I needed that.'"

The problems in Kansas City meant that Randy had to leave the large number of fans who stayed to meet him after the concert waiting while he ironed things out with the promoter. But as soon as that lengthy and unpleasant business was finished, he got back to doing what he is most interested in: meeting people one-on-one.

He talked and listened, joked and sympathized, and generally loved the people who waited more than an hour for the chance to meet him.

After all, that's why he is making Christian music in the first place.

Mom's Music, Norman's Kitchen, and Pat Boone's Help

Music and ministry weren't always connected in Randy's view of things. At first, this son of a Jewish father and Portuguese mother was just hooked on the music.

I've loved music for as long as I can remember. My mom loves to tell the story about when I was two years old. I would sit in front of the TV in my diapers watching "American Bandstand" and kick my foot to the beat of the drum. It astonished her, because I was really locked into the rhythm.

I started singing when I was four. My mom listened to a lot of folk music—the Weavers, the Kingston Trio, the Limelighters, and others, so I grew up listening to it. Pretty soon I was singing what I heard, and my neighbors would give me money to stop—no, seriously, they would give me pocket money to sing for them.

I started listening to Top 40 radio by the time I was eight, and by the time I was ten I was convinced I wanted to play guitar. My dad wanted me to play trumpet, and I explained to him that I couldn't sing and "honk" at the same time. So I talked him into getting me a guitar and starting guitar lessons.

Randy admits it wasn't the challenge of ministry that led him at age sixteen to grab his guitar, pack his notebook full of the songs he had been writing since age thirteen, and get on a jet for the first of many trips to Los Angeles. Rather, it was dreams of success and love.

Randy had been invited to L.A. by Larry Norman, who in 1969 made what is generally regarded as the first

Christian rock album and who promised to help Randy break into the music business, and Larry's sister Nancy who, Randy hoped, might fall madly in love with him. Instead, Randy was about to encounter a love beyond time and space.

As it turned out, Larry was out of town and Nancy was engaged to be married. But Randy hung in there. While waiting for Larry to return, he went to the College House, a youth outreach of Hollywood Presbyterian Church. There he saw young Christians up close.

"I really began to see the hand of God at work in Larry and the other people there," says Randy. "They blew my stereotype about church and religion out of the water because here were people putting their money where their mouths were—walking in faith and following the Bible."

But Randy, a skeptic, escaped unconverted and went back home to San Jose. "I was just about forgetting about Larry and this whole Christian experience when I got a letter from him."

Larry offered Randy another invitation to visit and Randy accepted. But this time, he was captured by the love of God.

It was August 12, 1970, and Larry and Randy were washing their lunch dishes.

Randy was not only a pioneer in Christian recorded music. His *Love Beyond Reason: The Video Album*, released in 1985, was the first Christian video album.

Larry asked me how I was doing, and that question just rang through the core of my being. This voice inside me said, *Yes, Randy, how are you doing?* I said, "I'm all right," but I wasn't sure I wanted to settle for all right all my life.

Larry told me later that he felt that would be the day I would turn my life over to God. He didn't really know what to say but he was obedient to God and God honored that.

Then he told me about God's love for me, and that I had everything to gain by giving Him my life, and nothing to lose. He asked me if I wanted to pray, and I said no. He looked sad. Then he waited a minute and asked if I wanted to pray yet. And then again.

I almost laughed at this, but the simplicity of the confrontation spoke to me. I just had to know if Jesus was who He said He was. That's news that's too wonderful to just make an uneducated guess about.

I said okay and Larry prayed a simple sinner's prayer. I said, "Lord, I don't know how to pray. I don't even know if I believe in You, but I believe in You enough to talk to You. If this outrageous love You demonstrated on the cross has anything to do with my life, I want it."

The Spirit really started to descend on the room, and I felt naked in the most permeating way I had ever felt. I couldn't wipe the grin off my face. I heaved a big sigh and a great weight left me; it was a weight I didn't even know I had been carrying. It was a very physical feeling, and I think God knew He had to do something really dramatic in my life. I was so used to tactile things—drugs and chasing girls—that God used the approach that if you hit the donkey over the head, you can get the donkey's attention and lead him wherever you want him to go.

Although it's been said you can lead a donkey to everlasting water but you can't make him drink, Randy drunk deeply of God. Pretty soon, songs like "Norman's Kitchen" began revealing Randy's newfound faith.

Randy and Larry became a two-man Christian rock scene: writing songs and playing at coffeehouses, churches, and college campuses. Randy recalls:

We looked around us and saw two things: First, we were completely alone. Nobody else was doing Christian rock music. And that was exciting. Second, we saw a real hunger in the eyes

of kids saying, "Look, I love the Lord but culturally the church leaves me cold. I've been raised in the sixties and I just don't relate to the church on a cultural level."

Our music talked about who they were in a way they could understand and in a language that could be understood by their friends, many of whom thought these young Christians had become Martians.

But still, we saw a vacuum. The music was happening on stage but there were no records. We wanted to be able to leave something at the concerts that would explain things more, so kids could take them home and say, "Mom, Dad, here's what I am and what is going on."

Unfortunately, the two Christian minstrels didn't have the money to finance their plans. For help they turned to Pat Boone.

Larry called Pat Boone, and we both went to his house. Though he was doing different things musically than we were, he was very broad-minded and realized that we could speak to a strata of the culture out there that he couldn't.

I can still remember Pat's four daughters sitting on the couch looking at us as we talked to their dad about our dreams. I think Debby was fourteen at the time. Pat listened to us and decided to help us out. He loaned us three thousand dollars so we could record my first album, and he let us use a studio he was involved in.

The album, *Born Twice*, was recorded for eight hundred dollars ("and it sounds like every penny of it, too," says Randy), half in the studio and half at a concert Randy gave at Westmont College in 1971 just five months after he had met the Lord. Fewer than ten thousand copies were made and today Christian vinyl collectors pay a premium for remaining copies. Some of the records were extra-special collector's editions: They had side one on both sides!

But even with its faults—or perhaps because of them—*Born Twice* is a musical time capsule of two things that would become more important in following years: the emerging Jesus Movement and the music of Randy Stonehill.

It is all there in his earliest songs—the vulnerable, trusting faith in God, the off-the-wall wit, along with the somber shades of the still young man. And, as the live side showed, the audience was eating it up.

That was just the beginning.

Funny Songs for Fallen People

One of the things that has endeared Randy Stonehill to his many fans in the fifteen years since his recording debut is his freshness in communicating Christian truths that may have become lost in two thousand years of tradition and rhetoric.

For modern listeners who might too easily dismiss songs that mention Christ or anything else that happened before 1960, Randy Stonehill is a uniquely gifted communicator. And one of the most popular and effective tools in his minstrel's kit is his humor. "I like to laugh," says Randy, who also likes to make other people laugh.

> I just keep my eyes open, and there are so many absurd and ludicrous things going on here in this arena we call modern civilization that I just can't resist poking fun at them.
>
> As I do that, I hope it would be in a loving and gentle way that might point out our inconsistencies and hypocrisies to the people who are listening, and in turn get us all to take a more honest look at ourselves and our need for God's truth, love, and wisdom in our lives.

Randy's lighter side can be seen in his 1976 song "Lung Cancer" which parodies cigarette smoking.

Randy's 1983 album, *Equator*, included attacks on two major American institutions, with "American Fast Food" taking on junk food:

> *Well, we're undernourished, but we're overfed*
> *And we're munching on the burger with the white bread*
> *And we're sucking up the sugar in the milkshake*
> *Til we slip into depression with a big headache*
> *And our arteries are crying out, "give us a break"*
>
> *American fast food, what a stupid way to die*
> *American fast food, kiss your old age good-bye*

And "Cosmetic Fixation" used an Elvis Costello-styled tune to attack not only beauty aids but the whole crazy cult of beauty and "looking out for number 1."

> *Cosmetic fixation, it's overtaking the nation*
> *Cosmetic fixation, it's such a sick situation*
> *Is her hair real blonde*
> *Are her legs real long*
> *Does she look real foxy on the party lawn*
> *You pretend your love is true*
> *But she's just a symbol of success to you*
>
> *Cosmetic fixation, we pursue it with dedication*
> *Cosmetic fixation, you know we use it like medication*
> *You got the foreign car*

Some of Randy's preconcert exercises involve adorning himself with any nearby prop.

> *With the phone and bar*
> *And the license plate says who you are*
> *You pretend you're satisfied*
> *Yes, but it's only there to stroke your pride*

In some of Randy's funny songs the effect is a mixed one: You don't know whether to laugh or cry.

"Christine," a plaintive, pretty ballad from 1981's *Between the Glory and the Flame* is about a man who falls in love with the local TV news anchorwoman. Although it seems like an absurd idea, the song achieves such a level of pathos that it's hard not to feel for this unhappy and lonely human.

> *I see you every night on channel seven, Christine*
> *like a vision in the silvery light*
> *and each day drags by so slowly till eleven, Christine*
> *how I hunger for your sight.*
>
> *now all my so-called friends they say that I'm a fool*
> *they say that you don't even know I'm there*
> *oh but they don't see that magic twinkle in your eye*
> *that special one that says how much you care*

Randy has explored the outer limits of humor like no other Christian artist, and these songs serve his purposes well. As he says in *Randy Stonehill, Words and Music,* a 1983 songbook:

"I'd like to think my songs act as mirrors that reflect the human condition: our fears, our hypocrisies, our hopes. I am convinced that when we begin to see ourselves more clearly, our need for forgiveness and salvation becomes painfully clear as well."

And Serious Songs Too

But hold on. Randy's more than a guitar-toting pundit. If you think some of his funny songs are serious, try his serious songs.

Try "Die Young" from . . . *Glory and the Flame,* for example. It's a strongly worded attack on the creeping nihilism that has become so fashionable in modern music and culture.

> the windows of the world
> are open wide tonight
> and everyone is dreaming
> 'neath the starry light
> but I can't sleep at all
> and dreams just waste my time
> I'll catch a thrill across the danger line

"And I used to dream of being a hero/Yeah, I told myself I'd never fall down."

> don't think about tomorrow
> it might never come
> have a good time and die young

Or take "Find Your Way to Me," from the same album:

> when your fears surround you
> when you're weary from the fight
> when your heart feels like an angry fist
> that pounds against the night
> there is Someone you can turn to
> oh there's Someone you should see
> little one you can find your way to Me

Like a thorough and conscientious novelist, Randy probes the deeper recesses and foibles of modern life, as in "Stop the World," from 1984's *Celebrate this Heartbeat:*

> We take our loftiest intentions
> And engrave them all neatly in stone
> And once they're safely up there
> We'd prefer that they just leave us alone
> 'Cause it's the law of the jungle
> With distinctly carnivorous vibes
> Yeah, we may dress up in tuxedos
> But we function like Germanic tribes
> It's the age-old sin in a modern day
> From the club of Cain to the laser ray
> Only now we can blow everybody away
> Stop the world I want to get off

Randy is a master at painting vivid song-pictures of lost people going deeper into despair. "Keep Me Running" is a taut, dynamic song that tells about a man desperately running from himself and his past.

Even an upbeat song like "Celebrate This Heartbeat" carries a note of urgency:

> I'm gonna celebrate this heartbeat
> Cause it just might be my last
> Every day is a gift from the Lord on high
> And they all go by so fast

It comes from the urgency Randy feels about life and his calling:

"I think there's room for both the lighter and the serious approaches. There's a time to be gentle but there's a time to shake somebody. I look at the things around me and I can't help wanting to shout, wanting to shake things up."

Fighting World Hunger

One issue that really gets Randy fighting mad and ready to shake people up is world hunger—the ever-present fact that forty-two thousand children die every day of hunger and hunger-related illnesses.

"After hearing about the problem and the ways I could help, I decided there was no excuse to sit back on my comfortable American sofa and pretend the tragedy of world hunger was not happening or pretend that I couldn't do anything about it."

Randy took action by sponsoring a young Haitian girl through Compassion International and then writing two powerful songs about the issue.

"Who Will Save the Children," from *Celebrate This Heartbeat*, tells of Randy's dawning awareness that real live children were dying through our neglect.

> *Cry for all the innocent ones*
> *Born into a world that's lost its heart*
> *For those who will never learn to dream*
> *Because their hope is crushed before they can start*
> *And we shake our fists at the air*
> *And say, "If God is love, how can this be fair?"*

The chorus tells of his decision to get off the sidelines and get involved:

> *But we are His hands, and we are His voice*
> *We are the ones who must make a choice*
> *And if it isn't now, tell me when?*
> *If it isn't you, then tell me*
> *Who will save the children?*

Randy visited Dana Pierre, the child he sponsors, in Haiti in 1984, and his increased awareness of the horrors of the child's life there were reflected in the final verse of "Judgement Day," from 1985's *Love Beyond Reason*.

> *The cruise ships painted white*
> *Are anchored in the bay*
> *The tourists fill their plates from the lunch buffet*
> *And the people on the shore*
> *Gazing up like silent ghosts*
> *Are doomed within a life*
> *That is worlds away*

For Randy, the experience was unforgettable:

> That trip to Haiti changed my whole life. Now when I think of the children in Haiti or Ethiopia I keep seeing my own three-year-old daughter's face in place of theirs and that really brings it all back home.

Randy visits with Dana Piere, the Haitian child he and his wife sponsor through Compassion International.

Oh, and we forgot to add, he's a committed rocker.

His *Love Beyond Reason* album and accompanying video show that even after turning thirty Randy still knows how to hook into the godly power of rock. Although he's sung his words to folk songs, ballads, fifties rock and sixties psychedelic rock, Jamaican spirituals, and other styles, it's rock that he returns to again and again.

Songs like "Angry Young Men," from *Love Beyond Reason*, show how expert Randy is at combining the power of God's love with the force of good rock.

> *He wants some angry young men*
> *Ones who can't be bought*
> *Ones who will not run from a fight*
> *Ones who will speak the truth whether it is popular or not*
> *Ones who'd give up anything to walk in His light*
>
> *Rest assured when Jesus comes again*
> *He'll be looking for some angry young men*

As Randy puts it:

> Rock is emotional, it's urgent, and it's simple. It's real gut-level music. When I sing I really try to give my heart back to God and the audience. I try to be transparent, and rock fits that bill.
>
> People respond to that. It's exciting and vital, and rock and roll is a wonderful vehicle for an audience to experience a genuine moment with you.
>
> And that's why rock and roll will never die—it connects with people on a real heart level.

When you see the children, all the cultural differences, political differences, racial differences, and any other kind of excuse you might be able to conjure up for why this happens melt away.

"Rock and Roll Will Never Die"

World hunger may be the issue Randy is most urgent about, but it is just one of the subjects of his work. He tackles the mentality that saves seals but kills unborn babies, asks an old friend to let bygones be bygones, challenges lukewarm Christians to return to their first love, and praises God for the wisdom and power to keep the whole globe together through another day's worth of heartbeats.

He also gives of himself in his work. Songs like "Letter to My Family," "Grandfather's Song," and "Turning Thirty" show that he is able to look inward as well as outward. Ask Randy if he's a sociologist, preacher, artist, performer, theologian, or crazy kind of guy and he'll say "all of the above."

"But above all of those things I am vulnerable. I am a vulnerable, real human being, struggling in faith, and if I can be that I think God honors that and breathes life and meaning into what I do."

Chapter Ten

AMY GRANT

It was the summer of 1980 and thousands of people, mostly teenagers, were sitting in the Florida sun listening to Amy Grant. The crowd at the Christian music festival was dressed for a day of music and sun—with most people wearing some version of shorts and summer tops.

Somehow the combination of heat, halter tops, and spiritual intimacy aroused the young people, setting a mood that could best be described as "sexually charged."

The then nineteen-year-old Miss Grant could feel the mood on stage and instead of ignoring it, dismissing it, or sticking to her "act," she confronted the problem head-on:

"I'm not married and I'm dying to have sex too," she said. "Sometimes I think, *If the line starts here let me be the first.* But we're making a commitment here."

It was a simple comment—showing her audience that she was susceptible to the same challenges and temptations they were, while reminding them of the commitment to holy living most of them shared.

But the comment said many things about Amy Grant who now, six years later, is the most popular Christian singer on the face of this earth, and still maintains a fresh, frank, and friendly approach to her music and her listeners.

From Church to Studio

Amy Grant has sold 4 million recordings of her unique brand of Christian pop/rock, but she didn't learn about rock music in the church where she grew up.

Born in Augusta, Georgia, and raised in Houston, Texas, Amy later moved with her family to Nashville where her father, a well-known doctor, took his wife and four daughters to the local Church of Christ. It was a conservative church which taught that the human voice—not musical instruments—should be used to praise God.

It was there that Amy dedicated her life to God and was baptized while she was in the seventh grade.

"I grew up in a Christian home," she says, "so I was really aware of God, knew all the Bible stories, and memorized Scriptures. And my parents weren't just church-goers; they were very sincere people."

Although her Christian home protected her from many dangers, it could not protect her from the doubts and questions she had two years later—the same feelings that would later help her write songs that reached others suffering similar times of testing.

> When I was a freshman in high school I thought, *Gee, Mom and Dad, I'm nuts about you, and I really love you, but I've got to figure this thing out for me.* They very graciously let me start going to the Belmont Church where my sisters had gone, which was sort of a remnant hippie group here in Nashville.
>
> It was wonderful. I could go in my jeans and bare feet, and there were girls in skimpy outfits. I thought, *If these people in this church will accept these crazy kids looking like this, then they can accept me.*
>
> Because even when you grow up in church all the time, you feel that everybody knows how rotten you are on the inside. If you're a "good kid" like I was, you never feel like you have tried and tested God's acceptance of you. But I *have* tried and tested the people in that church, and they really accepted me.
>
> Plus, the church really loved all kinds of people. There were prostitutes who worked in the area. People in the church prayed for them, and one night one of these girls came in and said, "I asked Jesus into my heart."
>
> Her testimony was a real scorcher—her language was foul and she didn't know any of the spiritual lingo—but in the middle of it all she said, "I have come to know that Jesus died for me."
>
> I was vicariously experiencing all of these things and it catapulted me, for the first time in my life, into a dramatic acceptance and exhilaration in my relationship with the Lord.
>
> And it was not quite a year after that I started writing songs.

While Grant's joy in her faith gave her the ideas for songs, the fifteen-year-old girl's notions of music came from the radio.

Grant listened to James Taylor, John Denver, Carole King, and others. But, as she told *USA Today,* "There were a lot of things happening in my life at that time that I felt I wanted to sing about, but nobody was writing about the things I was feeling. I needed something to fill out emotionally the missing pieces of the music that was already such a part of my life."

The way she filled in these musical gaps was by writing songs of her own—some of which she recorded on a cassette tape later that year.

> The summer before my junior year in high school I got a job working in a recording studio. It wasn't glamorous—I was vacuuming the floor, demagnetizing tape heads, and making labels for tapes. But I was doing exactly what I wanted to do.
>
> Without my knowing it, somebody had taken the tape I had made, called a record company, and played the tape over the phone. I had never sung for anybody but good friends, and suddenly it was my voice on this tape being scrutinized by tons of people.
>
> When they came to me and said, "This record company in Texas wants you to do a record," I was surprised, and so inhibited.

Grant signed a contract with Word Records at age fifteen and made plans for recording her debut album the following year. Her inhibitions were evident at the recording sessions where, to hide her fears, the seventeen-year-old Grant recorded the album with all lights off in a darkened studio.

Unwitting Superstar

Amy Grant didn't expect to become gospel music's most successful recording artist any more than she had expected people somewhere in Texas to listen to her tape over the phone and give her a contract. But when her album *Amy Grant* was released in 1977, it sold a healthy fifty thousand copies without Word or anybody else really doing much to promote it.

Amy's musical maturity, popularity, and record sales grew year by year with each new release: *My Father's Eyes, Never Alone,* two live albums, and the phenomenally popular *Age to Age.*

Since its release in 1982, *Age to Age* has become the first Christian-label release by a solo artist to "go platinum," selling more than a million copies to listeners of all ages, and winning a Grammy for Best Contemporary Gospel

Album and Dove Awards for Best Album and Cover of the Year.

Grant's next release, *A Christmas Album*, "went gold" (for sales of half a million units) in the winter of 1985. Her 1984 release, *Straight Ahead*, continued to reflect her growth as an artist and her importance to the gospel music industry, going gold in 1985.

While Grant's recordings have been racking up such strong sales figures, she has also been playing to large crowds in halls and auditoriums around the country, mixing her music with warm and honest chats with her audiences.

During her fall 1984 tour of the Northeast she sold out Radio City Music Hall in New York City, the Centrum in Boston, and the Spectrum in Philadelphia. *Rolling Stone* magazine reported that in 1984 Grant performed for half a million people. She played for closer to a million people in 1985 and plans to sing to thousands more in 1986.

Through it all, the still-young singer has kept her wits and humility intact. In fact, she seems as surprised by all the hullabaloo as anyone, and she's not just reading from some script for Christian celebrities when she lays the credit for her stunning success at the feet of her Lord.

> I don't think about whether or not I'm a super-star. In fact, I haven't been very enamored with that phrase, even before I started singing. For some onlookers it is very important to say, "I really like Amy Grant and she's popular," or for some young person to say, "She's a star."
>
> I can think of one little girl who was so precious. She had met me backstage at a concert in Lakeland, Florida, and she was looking for my door. On the door was a little piece of paper with my name scribbled on it held to the door with masking tape.
>
> I saw her at a later concert at Disneyworld, and she had a present for me—a door plaque with my name and a star on it. She looked at me and said, "I was crushed when I came backstage and saw that all you had was a little piece of paper with your name scribbled on it." It hadn't bothered me that much but for her it was important to say, "You are important to me."
>
> Celebrity status is only as important as the person who is listening to you thinks it is. I'm going to sing regardless, whether anybody listens or not.

But even when it comes to singing, Grant doesn't claim any monopoly on God-given talents. "I can sing," she told Nashville writer Neil Pond, "but I know there are a

Amy picks up her 1985 Grammy Award for Best Gospel Performance for her song "Angels."

lot of people sitting around singing backup sessions who can sing circles around me. And why they're doing backup sessions and I'm singing to ten thousand people in Dallas, Texas, I don't know.

"I think that whenever there's that incomprehensible element, that one thing that you can't put your finger on, you can't tell why it's working . . . I really feel it's a blessing from the Lord."

No Sexpot for Jesus

Amy Grant's intimate autobiographical writing style, which takes events from her daily life and turns them into modern Christian classics, has made her thousands of friends among young believers who identify with her struggles in living the Christian life.

Her down-home southern drawl charms audiences of rapt concertgoers who hang on the singer's every word.

Her natural-looking attractiveness helps Grant sell albums and gain prominent coverage in large-circulation national newspapers, like USA Today, and magazines, like Parade and People.

Her refreshing performances earn her spots on nationally televised specials, like Patti Labelle's show on Thanksgiving Day 1985, and the Martin Luther King special in early 1986.

Her presence is equally refreshing on television talk shows. In early 1986 Grant, along with Andrae Crouch and others, appeared on Phil Donahue's show. She sang husband Gary's composition, "Father's Eyes," and discussed her vocation.

It may not have been as controversial as the show on sexual dominance and submission Phil had hosted two days earlier, but the people in the audience seemed to like what Grant was doing. "Your records have replaced Ozzy Osborne in my house," said one mother.

And her refreshing, hope-filled approach to the Christian life has attracted both believers and nonbelievers to her music and her message.

But controversy follows celebrity, and one aspect of the Amy Grant phenomenon that has raised eyebrows in the church is her unapologetically vibrant sexuality.

Some conservative Christians see Grant—barefoot, singing and dancing on the 1985 Grammy Awards telecast—and they wonder what this has to do with the gospel. Others blush at Grant's frank comments about sex such as those that opened this chapter.

But surprisingly, much of the criticism comes not from the pulpit but from the papers. Richard Harrington of the Washington Post wrote that Grant "is projecting a confusingly sexy image for an avowedly spiritual singer," while the New York Times's John Rockwell went further, writing

of Grant's "deliberately alluring, even sexy publicity photos, hand on thigh and jeans rolled up to mid-calf."

Of course one might ask Mr. Rockwell, who covers popular music for the Times, how Grant's calves can be called "sexy" in the context of artists like Madonna and Prince who leave little to the imagination. But Grant's attractiveness and, perhaps more, her comfort with her own attractiveness, has astonished many religious and secular critics.

Asked about the criticism, Grant seems surprised—even embarrassed. "I don't choose any of those pictures," she said, referring to the Straight Ahead shots that so surprised Mr. Rockwell, "and the people who chose the pictures were fun-loving and innocent."

> Obviously, anybody in management for a Christian record company would only want to engender a positive response. The last thing they would want to do is say, "Hey, we've got a sexpot singing about Jesus."
>
> We probably took two thousand pictures that day. I was in front of the camera for nine hours, and we got crazy. We took off our shoes, stood on our heads, and jumped up and down.
>
> When they chose the shots they probably thought, This is fun; this is free. This is somebody who is uninhibited. She looks kind of silly, and she's leaning over. I think it was a total misunderstanding that it was supposed to be sexy.

But even though some have raised questions and eyebrows over Grant's good looks, she remains a solid Christian role model for young people struggling with today's sex-charged climate. Her lyrics are about love for God and other people. And she seems certain of the difference between love and lust.

In her own life Grant has followed the Christian teachings on dating and marriage. Unlike Madonna, who twisted the words "Like a Virgin" in new and saddening ways, Grant reported to People magazine that she was a virgin when she married Gary Chapman in 1982. And hardly anybody doubted her.

Since her marriage to Chapman, who writes some of Grant's songs and plays rhythm guitar in her band, Grant has shown that couples can stick it out together, proving to thousands of young listeners that love and faithfulness aren't just the stuff of fairy tales or ancient, repressive societies.

After all, Grant seems to ask, what better way is there to expose the emptiness of the "sex is everything" philosophy espoused in much of modern music than by showing Christians who follow God's commands and enjoy their sexuality just as God intended it to be?

Some people, though, prefer silence over frankness and would rather ignore the subject of sexuality than have an attractive, popular singer bring it up in concerts and interviews.

Some of the strongest criticism of Grant's straight talk came after an article about her in *Rolling Stone*. It was the first time that magazine had profiled a Christian-label recording artist.

Grant was far from prudish in the three days of interviews that went into the article. She told *Rolling Stone* writer Michael Goldberg that she had normal sex drives ("My hormones are just as on key as any other twenty-four-year-old's") and tried to communicate the glory of human sexuality as God intended it to be in the Garden of Eden ("I feel that a Christian young woman in the eighties is *very* sexual").

Grant raised more Christian eyebrows and temperatures when she described her disgust with the obscenity she saw in a concert performance by the seemingly sex-obsessed Prince ("I didn't get off watching him create an illusion of masturbating").

But she caught the most heat and criticism with a phrase that wasn't even hers: In a paragraph where she talked about how marriage was the place for sex, Grant was quoted as saying, "But I see sex not just as a way [to get release] but to say, this is an integral part of our working relationship."

According to Melinda Scruggs, who has worked with Grant in the Nashville offices of Blanton–Harrell Productions for five years, the colorful phrase attributed to Amy belonged to interviewer Goldberg, not the singer.

"Because Amy is ten times more visible than most of us, her mistakes and problems are ten times more visible than ours," says Scruggs.

Don Finto, the pastor of the Belmont Church where Amy and Gary Chapman fellowship, says, "Sometimes Amy is not always wise in the way she says things, but I really do believe she's where God wants her to be.

"Amy desires to be a full person—to be sexual in a godly sense. She doesn't want to be a sex symbol, but wants sex to be seen as a good thing, a godly thing."

Ours might be a better world if sex wasn't a major cultural preoccupation both for teens and adults. But ours was the world Grant was born into, and attacking false views of sex is a part of her ministry, as is telling her listeners that Jesus loves them.

For Those Who Have Ears to Hear

In 1985, with the release of *Unguarded*, Grant's ministry/career took a new and exciting turn.

Earlier in the year Word Records, Grant's Christian record company, signed a deal with A&M Records, allowing A&M to take *Unguarded* and other Word albums to the mainstream. With *Unguarded* in both secular and Christian shops, it took off—going gold in forty-five days (and promising to go platinum in 1986).

"Find a Way," the album's first single, was a national Top 40 hit, another gospel first, and could be heard on radios, in shopping malls, and on beaches throughout the land. Later singles from *Unguarded*, "Wise Up" and "Everywhere I Go," though, failed to make a similar impact on the national charts and consciousness.

Unguarded did well on *Billboard*'s Top 200 Albums chart, staying on the list for thirty-eight consecutive weeks.

John Styll, publisher of *Contemporary Christian Magazine* and *Musicline*, expressed the excitement as well as anyone:

> Amy Grant's "Find a Way" is the first song by an artist signed to a Christian label to show up on *Billboard*'s "Hot 100" chart. [*Unguarded*] is also the first [album] to make a major dent on that magazine's LP chart.
>
> Many media opportunities continue to come her way, and in every case she presents herself as a contemporary artist with a message. If that's not being "salty" in today's world, I don't know what is.

But again, controversy followed celebrity, and some Christians were unhappy with what Grant and her records were up to.

Many Christians agreed with the tone of this letter, which appeared in *Contemporary Christian Magazine*: "I'm deeply saddened that you would perpetuate the career of Amy Grant, who seems determined to besmirch fundamental Christian values."

At the same time, many people who didn't listen to Christian radio or weren't in the habit of shopping for records in Christian bookstores were finally discovering Grant, such as the woman who wrote the following letter to *Rolling Stone*: "I found your article on Amy Grant very interesting, refreshing, and inspiring. So inspiring, in fact, that I went out and bought her latest recording, *Unguarded*. I find her style of music up-to-date and, after listening to hard-core rock for the past few years, a very welcome change."

Aside from the deal with A&M, there are other things that have helped *Unguarded* do so well in the secular market. One is the skill and obvious care with which the album was recorded. *Unguarded* cost $200,000 to record, and employed talented studio musicians like drummer Paul Leim; bassist Mike Brignardello; guitarists Dann Huff, Michael Landau, and Jon Goin (Chapman didn't play on the album); and keyboardists Michael W. Smith and Robbie Buchanan, who have become regulars on Grant's records.

Unguarded has a harder rock edge, making it a more likely candidate for secular airplay. It also shows the latest stage in the evolution of Grant's songwriting. Whereas her early albums focused solely on salvation and other Christian messages for believers, *Unguarded* is not, as Grant says, "paraphrases of John 3:16," but instead, "observations of everyday life from a Christian perspective."

Grant described the insight (she wanted to say *vision*, but that "sounds so super-spiritual") that guided her writing for *Unguarded*:

> Having passed the one hundred-song mark in my writing, I found myself really thinking hard about how I could creatively communicate Jesus. With this being the ninth album I felt like the old lady in the shoe who had already said it all.
>
> But I started reading about when Jesus was communicating with the masses, and how so often He would say something really deep—really heavy—but it was almost cloaked. And then He would go away and explain it fully to His disciples. And I thought, *Lord, is there really something to that? Do we sometimes try so hard to explain You that we remove the mystery?*
>
> And kids who are trying to find out what's really happening in this life look at somebody who is presenting all the answers and they think, *There's no search here. They're already telling me everything. There's no looking; there's no finding.*
>
> So I found that the lyrics of this new album started not saying everything. And it wasn't an effort to say I'm not going to say *Jesus*. But it was an effort to say, "You know what? I want to allow a little bit of the mystery of God to be in this album."

Although Grant wanted to leave room for mystery on *Unguarded*, it's no mystery what motivates the lady who sings the lyrics to "Love of Another Kind," the album's opening song:

They say love is cruel
They say love is rather fragile
But I've found in You
A love of another kind

The song's chorus goes on to identify the person identified only as "You" in the verse: "Jesus' love is like no other."

In "Find a Way," Grant sings this bridge:

If our God His Son not sparing
Came to rescue you
Is there any circumstance
That He can't see you through

All in all, three of the ten songs on *Unguarded* mention Jesus, with a fourth that calls Jesus "He." Eight of the songs communicate strong Christian messages (like the single, "Wise Up"—"Better wise up / Better think twice / Never leave room for compromise"). On the album's liner notes, five of the songs are introduced with passages from the Bible.

With *Unguarded*, Grant answers the question she asked in a 1983 article in *People* magazine:

"It's like there's a huge mountain called the music business, and this thing next to it, a little bitty saltshaker—that's the Christian music business. My question is, how can I sing to that mountain of people out there?"

Grant is finding out how to reach that mountain, and even though some in the church question her motives and her approach, she presses on.

For, at a time when Christians and others are concerned about the obscene and evil lyrics of popular music, Grant is singing songs of life and truth. At a time when many Christians are up in arms about what popular records say when played backwards, Grant is singing *forwards* about God's Son.

And at a time when rock's Pied Pipers seduce young people to wink at sin, Grant is pointing toward a better Way.

DISCOGRAPHY

Mylon LeFevre

We Believe, 1970 (Cotillion, SC 9026)
Mylon With Holy Smoke, 1971 (Columbia, C 31085)
Over the Influence, 1972 (Columbia, KC 31472)
Weak at the Knees, 1977 (Warner Brothers, BS 3070)
Love Rustler, 1978 (Warner Brothers, BSK 3216)
Rock & Roll Resurrection, 1979 (Mercury, SRM-1-3799)

Alvin Lee and Mylon LeFevre
On the Road to Freedom, 1973 (Columbia, C 32729)

Mylon LeFevre & Broken Heart
Mylon LeFevre & Broken Heart, 1982 (MCA, MRC 5021)
More, 1983 (Myrrh, MSB 6753)
Live Forever, 1983 (Myrrh, SPCN 7-01-6758-06-0)
Sheep in Wolves Clothing, 1985 (Myrrh, SPCN 7-01-6790-06-1/A&M, SP 752)

Resurrection Band / Rez Band

Awaiting Your Reply, 1978 (Star Song, SSR 0011)
Rainbow's End, 1979 (Star Song, SSR 0015)
Colours, 1980 (Light, LS 5783)

Mommy Don't Love Daddy Anymore, 1981 (Light, LS 5803)
DMZ, 1982 (Light, LS 5816)
Bootleg Live, 1984 (Sparrow, SPR 1086/Capitol, ST 41014)
Hostage, 1984 (Sparrow, SPR 1099/Capitol, ST 41018)
Between Heaven 'n' Hell, 1985 (Sparrow, SPR 1111/Capitol, ST 41024)

Jessy Dixon

It's All Right Now, 1977 (Light, LS 5719)
You Bring Out the Sun, 1979 (Light, LS 5747)
Satisfied/Live, 1982 (Light, LS 5797)
Sanctuary, 1983 (Power Discs, PWR 01072)
Silent Partner, 1985 (Power Discs, PWR 01078)

Leslie Phillips

Beyond Saturday Night, 1983 (Myrrh, MSB 6743/A&M, WR 8189)
Dancing With Danger, 1984 (Myrrh, SPCN 7-10-680206-X/A&M, WR 8148)

Black and White in a Grey World, 1985 (Myrrh LA, SPCN 7-01-682606-6/A&M, WR 8313)

Michael Omartian

White Horse, 1975 (ABC/Myrrh, MSA 6564)
Adams Again, 1976 (Myrrh, MSA 6576)
Conversations, 1986 (Meadowlark, MLR 7008 [Sparrow], ML 41042 [Capitol])

Michael and Stormie Omartian
Seasons of the Soul, 1978 (Myrrh, MSB 6006)
The Builder, 1980 (Myrrh, MSB 6636)
Odyssey (The Best of), 1981 (Myrrh, MSB 6731)
Mainstream, 1982 (Sparrow, SPR 1060)
Together Live (with Second Chapter of Acts), 1983 (Sparrow, SPR 1068)

Stormie Omartian
Exercise for Life, 1982 (Sparrow, SPR 1064)
Exercise for Life, Vol. II, 1983 (Sparrow, SPR 1082)

Stryper

The Yellow and Black Attack, 1984 (Enigma, E 1064)
Soldiers Under Command, 1985 (Enigma, 72077)

Steve Taylor

I Want to Be a Clone, 1982 (Sparrow, SPR 1063/Capitol, SQ 4100)
Meltdown Remixes, 1984 (Sparrow, SPR 1100)
Meltdown, 1984 (Sparrow, SPR 1083/Capitol, ST 41013)
Transatlantic Remix (with Sheila Walsh), 1985 (Sparrow, SPR 1107)
On the Fritz, 1985 (Sparrow, SPR 1105/Capitol, ST 41023)
Limelight, 1986 (Sparrow, SPR 1118/Capitol, SQ 41035)

Petra

Petra, 1974 (Myrrh, MST 6527/A&M, SP 5061)
Come and Join Us, 1977 (Myrrh, MSB 6582/A&M, SP 5062)

Washes Whiter Than, 1979 (Star Song, SSR 0014/A&M, SP 5063)
Never Say Die, 1981 (Star Song, SSR 0032/A&M, SP 5064)
More Power to Ya, 1982 (Star Song, SSR 0045/A&M, SP 5065)
Not of This World, 1983 (Star Song, SPCN 7-102-05086-0/A&M, SP 5066)
Beat the System, 1984 (Star Song, SPCN 7-102-05786-5/A&M, SP 5067)
Captured in Time and Space, 1986 (Star Song [2 LP] SPCN 7-102-06586-8/A&M, SP 6104)

Randy Stonehill

Born Twice, 1971
Welcome to Paradise, 1976 (Solid Rock, SRA 2002)
The Sky Is Falling, 1980 (Solid Rock, SRA 2005)
Between the Glory and the Flame, 1981 (Myrrh, MSB 6679)
Equator, 1983 (Myrrh, MSB 6742/A&M, WR 8222)
Celebrate This Heartbeat, 1984 (Myrrh, SPCN 7-01-676506-7/A&M, WR 8130)
Love Beyond Reason, 1985 (Myrrh, SPCN 7-01-681106-9/A&M, WR 8304)

Amy Grant

Amy Grant, 1978 (Myrrh, MSB 6586/A&M, SP 5051)
My Father's Eyes, 1979 (Myrrh, MSB 6625/A&M, SP 5052)
Never Alone, 1980 (Myrrh, MSB 6645/A&M, SP 5053)
Amy Grant in Concert, 1981 (Myrrh, MSB 6668/A&M, SP 5054)
In Concert, Vol. II, 1981 (Myrrh, MSB 6677/A&M, SP 5055)
**Age to Age*, 1982 (Myrrh, MSB 6697/A&M, SP 5056)
A Christmas Album, 1983 (Myrrh, SPCN 7-01-676806-6/A&M, SP 5057)
Straight Ahead, 1984 (Myrrh, SPCN 7-01-675706-4/A&M, SP 5058)
**Unguarded*, 1985 (Myrrh, SPCN 7-01-680606-5/A&M, SP 5060)

* Certified Gold (sale of half a million units)
** Certified Platinum (sale of 1 million units)

LYRIC CREDITS

"Amazing" by Glenn Kaiser and Jim Denton, © Copyright 1980 LUMINAR MUSIC (SESAC).

"American Fast Food" by Randy Stonehill, © Copyright 1983 Stonehillian Music and Word Music (A Div. of WORD, INC.).

"American Dream" by Jon Trott, Glenn Kaiser, Jim Denton, and Stu Heiss, © Copyright 1980 LUMINAR MUSIC (SESAC).

"Angel of Light" by Bob Hartman, © Copyright 1981 Dawn Treader Music (SESAC). Administered by Gaither Music Company.

"Angry Young Men" by Randy Stonehill, © Copyright 1985 Stonehillian Music and Word Music (A Div. of WORD, INC.).

"Area 312" by Jon Trott, Wendi Kaiser, Stu Heiss, and Jim Denton, © Copyright 1982 LUMINAR MUSIC (SESAC).

"Beat the System" by Bob Hartman, © Copyright 1985 Dawn Treader Music (SESAC). Administered by Gaither Music Company.

"Black and White in a Grey World" by Leslie Phillips, © Copyright 1985 Word Music (A Div. of WORD, INC.).

"Bring Me Through" by Leslie Phillips, © Copyright 1981 Maranatha! Music.

"By My Spirit" by Leslie Phillips, © Copyright 1984 Word Music (A Div. of WORD, INC.).

"Celebrate the Lord" by John Elliott and Mark Baldwin, © Copyright 1985 Laurel Press, a division of Lorenz Creative Services/Charlie Monk Music, Nashville, TN.

"Celebrate This Heartbeat" by Randy Stonehill, © Copyright 1984 Stonehillian Music and Word Music (A Div. of WORD, INC.).

"Chameleon" by Bob Hartman, © Copyright 1981 Dawn Treader Music (SESAC). Administered by Gaither Music Company.

"Christine" by Randy Stonehill, © Copyright 1981 Stonehillian Music and Word Music (A Div. of WORD, INC.).

"City Streets" by Glenn Kaiser, Jon Trott, and Jim Denton, © Copyright 1980 LUMINAR MUSIC (SESAC).

"Colours" by Glenn Kaiser, © Copyright 1980 LUMINAR MUSIC (SESAC).

"Cosmetic Fixation" by Randy Stonehill, © Copyright Stonehillian Music and Word Music (A Div. of WORD, INC.).

"Crimes" by Glenn Kaiser, © Copyright Rez Band Music.

"Dancing With Danger" by Leslie Phillips, © Copyright 1984 Word Music (A Div. of WORD, INC.).

"Defective Youth" by Jon Trott, © Copyright Rez Band Music.

"Die Young" by Randy Stonehill, © Copyright 1981 Stonehillian Music and Word Music (A Div. of WORD, INC.).

"Dr. Jesus" by Michael and Stormie Omartian, © Copyright 1980 See This House Music and Word Music (A Div. of WORD, INC.).

"Elevator Muzik" by Glenn Kaiser, © Copyright 1981 LUMINAR MUSIC (SESAC).

"Fat City" by Michael and Stormie Omartian, © Copyright 1974 MCA MUSIC (A Division of MCA, INC.) and HOLICANTHUS MUSIC, New York, NY.

"Find a Way" by Michael W. Smith and Amy Grant, © Copyright 1985 Meadowgreen Music Co./Bug & Bear Music. Meadowgreen adm. by Tree Pub. Co., Inc. 8 Music Sq. W., Nashville, TN 37203. Bug & Bear Music exclusive adm. LCS Music Group, Inc. P.O. Box 202406, Dallas, TX 75220.

"Find Your Way to Me" by Randy Stonehill, © Copyright 1981 Stonehillian Music and Word Music (A Div. of WORD, INC.).

"For the Record" by Mylon LeFevre, © Copyright Upfall Music Corp./St. Lucifer Music/Holy Smoke Music (ASCAP).

"From Wrong to Right" by Michael Sweet, Robert Sweet, and Oz Fox, © Copyright 1984 Bug Music/Amgine Music (BMI).

"The Gods of Men" by Randy Stonehill, © Copyright 1985 Stonehillian Music and Word Music (A Div. of WORD, INC.).

"Guilty by Association" by Steve Taylor, © Copyright 1983 C.A. Music/Birdwing Music/Cherry Lane Music Publishing Co., Inc.

"He Really Didn't Have to Die" by Jessy Dixon, © Copyright 1982 LEXICON MUSIC, INC. (ASCAP).

"Hero" by Steve Taylor, © Copyright 1983 C.A. Music/Birdwing Music/Cherry Lane Music Publishing Co., Inc.

"He's Not Just a Soldier" by Richard Penniman and William Pitt, © Copyright Woodman Music Publishing Company.

"Hollow Eyes" by Bob Hartman, © Copyright 1985 Dawn Treader Music (SESAC). Administered by Gaither Music Company.

"Holy Smoke Doo Dah Band" by Mylon LeFevre and Auburn Burrell, © Copyright Windfall Music, Inc./St. Lucifer Music/Mylon LeFevre Music (BMI).

"I'll Remember You" by Randy Stonehill, © Copyright 1984 Stonehillian Music and Word Music (A Div. of WORD, INC.).

"I Manipulate" by Steve Taylor, © Copyright 1985 C.A. Music/Birdwing Music.

"It's You" by Jon Trott, © Copyright Rez Band Music.

"I Want to Be a Clone" by Steve Taylor, © Copyright 1982 C.A. Music/Birdwing Music/Cherry Lane Music Publishing Co., Inc.

"I Won't Let It Come Between Us" by Leslie Phillips, © Copyright 1984 Word Music (A Div. of WORD, INC.).

"Jeremiah" by Michael and Stormie Omartian, © Copyright 1974 MCA MUSIC (A Division of MCA, INC.) and HOLICANTHUS MUSIC, New York, NY.

"Judgement Day" by Randy Stonehill, © Copyright 1985 Stonehillian Music and Word Music (A Div. of WORD, INC.).

"Killing My Old Man" by Bob Hartman, © Copyright 1981 Dawn Treader Music (SESAC). Administered by Gaither Music Company.

"Lifeboat" by Steve Taylor, © Copyright 1985 C.A. Music/Birdwing Music.

"Light of Love" by Leslie Phillips, © Copyright 1984 Word Music (A Div. of WORD, INC.).

"Loud 'n' Clear" by Michael Sweet, © Copyright 1984 Bug Music/Amgine Music (BMI).

"Love of Another Kind" by Richard Mullins, Wayne Kirkpatrick, Amy Grant, and Gary Chapman, © Copyright 1984 Meadowgreen Music Co./River Oaks Music Co./Bug & Bear Music/Fred & Ethel Music Co., Inc. Meadowgreen & River Oaks adm. by Tree Pub. Co., Inc., 8 Music Square W., Nashville, TN 37203. Bug & Bear Music exclusive adm. LCS Music Group, Inc. P.O. Box 202406, Dallas, TX 75220.

"Makes Me Wanna Sing" by Michael Sweet, © Copyright 1985 Sweet Family Music.

"Meat the Press" by Steve Taylor, © Copyright 1983 C.A. Music/Birdwing Music/Cherry Lane Music Publishing Co., Inc.

"Meltdown (At Madame Tussaud's)" by Steve Taylor, © Copyright 1983 C.A. Music/Birdwing Music/Cherry Lane Music Publishing Co., Inc.

"Mommy Don't Love Daddy Anymore" by Glenn Kaiser and Jon Trott, © Copyright 1981 LUMINAR MUSIC (SESAC).

"The More I Know You" by Leslie Phillips, © Copyright 1985 Word Music (A Div. of WORD, INC.).

"Mr. Trash Man" by Michael and Stormie Omartian, © Copyright 1980 See This House Music and Word Music (A Div. of WORD, INC.).

"Ms. Past" by Stormie Omartian, © Copyright See This House Music (ASCAP).

"My Heart Belongs to Him" by Bill Morris, Dean Harrington, and Mylon LeFevre, © Copyright Angel Band Music (BMI).

"Nervous World" by Glenn and Wendi Kaiser, © Copyright Rez Band Music.

"Never Say Die" by Bob Hartman, © Copyright 1981 Dawn Treader Music (SESAC). Administered by Gaither Music Company.

"N.Y.C." by Glenn Kaiser and Jim Denton, © Copyright 1980 LUMINAR MUSIC (SESAC).

"One Song Is Not Enough" by Michael and Stormie Omartian, © Copyright 1982 See This House Music/Birdwing Music/Cherry Lane Music Publishing Co., Inc.

"Playground" by Jim Denton and Jon Trott, © Copyright Rez Band Music

"Praise Ye the Lord" by Greg X. Volz, © Copyright 1981 Dawn Treader Music (SESAC). Administered by Gaither Music Company.

"Railroad Angels" by Mylon LeFevre, © Copyright Mylon LeFevre Music (BMI).

"The Rock That Makes Me Roll" by Michael Sweet, © Copyright 1985 Sweet Family Music.

"Silver Fish" by Michael and Stormie Omartian © Copyright 1974 MCA MUSIC (A Division of MCA, INC.) and HOLICANTHUS MUSIC, New York, NY.

"Sin for a Season" by Steve Taylor, © Copyright 1983 C.A. Music/Birdwing Music/Cherry Lane Music Publishing Co., Inc.

"Soldiers Under Command" by Michael Sweet and Robert Sweet, © Copyright 1985 Sweet Family Music.

"Song in the Night" by Leslie Phillips, © Copyright 1984 Word Music (A Div. of WORD, INC.).

"Stark/Spare" by Glenn Kaiser and Stu Heiss, © Copyright 1981 LUMINAR MUSIC (SESAC).

"Steeplechase" by Steve Taylor, © Copyright 1982 C.A. Music/Birdwing Music/Cherry Lane Music Publishing Co., Inc.

"Stop the World" by Randy Stonehill, © Copyright 1984 Stonehillian Music and Word Music (A Div. of WORD, INC.).

"Stranger to Danger" by Mylon LeFevre and Dean Harrington, © Copyright Angel Band Music (BMI).

"Strength of My Life" by Leslie Phillips, © Copyright 1984 Word Music (A Div. of WORD, INC.).

"The Struggle" by Glenn Kaiser, Jim Denton, and Stu Heiss, © Copyright 1980 LUMINAR MUSIC (SESAC).

"Sunday School Blues" by Mylon LeFevre, Kim Venable, and Auburn Burrell, © Copyright Mylon LeFevre Music (BMI).

"Surrender" by Michael Sweet, © Copyright 1985 Sweet Family Music.

"Sweet Peace Within" by Mylon LeFevre and Steve Sanders, © Copyright Mylon LeFevre Music (BMI).

"Take Me Down" by Michael and Stormie Omartian, © Copyright 1974 MCA MUSIC (A Division of MCA, INC.) and HOLICANTHUS MUSIC, New York, NY.

"This Disco (Used to Be a Cute Cathedral)" by Steve Taylor, © Copyright 1985 C.A. Music/Birdwing Music.

"Through the Blood" by Jessy Dixon, © Copyright 1982 LEXICON MUSIC, INC. (ASCAP).

"Travel on With Me" by Stormie Omartian, © Copyright See This House Music (ASCAP).

"2000" by Glenn and Wendi Kaiser, © Copyright Rez Band Music.

"Understand It" by Mylon LeFevre, © Copyright Angel Band Music (BMI).

"Walking in the Light" by Bob Hartman, © Copyright 1974 Petsong Publishing.

"The Warrior" by Stan Coates and Mylon LeFevre, © Copyright Angel Band Music/Dayspring (BMI).

"Waves" by Glenn Kaiser, © Copyright 1978 Dawn Treader Music (SESAC). Administered by Gaither Music Company.

"Waymaker" by Mylon LeFevre, © Copyright Upfall Music Corp./St. Lucifer Music/Holy Smoke Music (ASCAP).

"We Don't Need No Colour Code" by Steve Taylor, © Copyright 1983 C.A. Music/Birdwing Music/Cherry Lane Music Publishing Co., Inc.

"Whachersign" by Michael and Stormie Omartian, © Copyright 1975 MCA MUSIC (A Division of MCA, INC.) and HOLICANTHUS MUSIC, New York, NY.

"When the World Is New" by Leslie Phillips, © Copyright 1985 Word Music (A Div. of WORD, INC.).

"Where I Been" by Stormie Omartian, © Copyright See This House Music (ASCAP).

"Who Knows" by Mylon LeFevre, Kim Venable, and Auburn Burrell, © Copyright Mylon LeFevre Music (BMI).

"Who's Real Anymore" by Jim Denton, © Copyright Rez Band Music.

"Who Will Save the Children" by Randy Stonehill, © Copyright 1984 Stonehillian Music and Word Music (A Div. of WORD, INC.).

"Wise Up" by Billy Simon and Wayne Kirkpatrick, © Copyright 1984 Meadowgreen Music Co./River Oaks Music Co. All rights adm. by Tree Pub. Co., Inc., 8 Music Square W., Nashville, TN 37203.

"Without Him" by Mylon LeFevre, © Copyright 1963 LeFevre-Sing Publishing.

"Without Him We Can Do Nothing" by Greg X. Volz, © Copyright 1981 Dawn Treader Music (SESAC). Administered by Gaither Music Company.

"You Don't Owe Me Nothing" by Steve Taylor, © Copyright 1985 C.A. Music/Birdwing Music.

"You Know What to Do" by Michael Sweet, Robert Sweet, Oz Fox, and Tim Gaines, © Copyright 1984 Bug Music/Amgine Music (BMI).

"You're Still on His Mind" by Mylon LeFevre, © Copyright Mylon LeFevre Music (BMI).

"Your Kindness" by Leslie Phillips, © Copyright 1985 Word Music (A Div. of WORD, INC.).

"You've Been Bought" by Steve Taylor, © Copyright 1985 C.A. Music/Birdwing Music.